Herodotus
THE PERSIAN WARS: A COMPANION

HERODOTUS
The Persian Wars

A Companion to the Penguin translation
of Books 5–9 from *Herodotus: The
Histories*, translated by Aubrey de
Sélincourt, published in the Penguin
Classics

With Introduction and Commentary by
Stephen Usher

Published by Bristol Classical Press
General Editor: John H. Betts

Cover illustration: Herodotus, from a portrait bust, Dresden.
[Drawing by Emma Faull.]

First published in 1988 by
Bristol Classical Press
an imprint of
Gerald Duckworth & Co. Ltd
The Old Piano Factory
48 Hoxton Square, London N1 6PB

Reprinted 1994

A catalogue record for this book is available
from the British Library

ISBN 1-85399-030-2

Available in USA and Canada from:
Focus Information Group
PO Box 369
Newburyport
MA 01950

Printed in Great Britain by
Booksprint, Bristol

Contents

Preface

In order to concentrate on the central theme of Herodotus' *History*, the Persian Wars, it has been necessary to select certain passages from Books 5 and 6 (5.28–38, 49–51, 97–125; 6.1–21, 94–136), and to pay more attention to some parts of the narrative than to others in the continuous coverage of Books 7, 8 and 9. Like its predecessor in this series, Thomas Wiedemann's commentary on Thucydides 1–2.65, the present commentary is keyed to the translation in the Penguin Classics series, which was made by Aubrey de Slincourt in 1954 and revised by A.R. Burn in 1972. The latter's excellent introduction has enabled me to avoid repetition in my own, and to dwell on a small number of points which seem especially important.

The commentary will have served its purpose if it encourages students to read Herodotus with greater enjoyment and a better appreciation of his position both as a pioneer and a master of the art of writing history. Some will be impressed by his curiosity, and wish to emulate it by reading what others have written about him. They will find enough reference to modern research to satisfy their immediate needs, and they will also find that Herodotus emerges from this scholarly examination with an enhanced reputation.

With first-hand knowledge of the students expected to use this book, BCP's reader has been able to make some constructive suggestions, and BCP's editor, Mr. Kim Richardson, has seen it through to completion with patience and care. My thanks also go to Christine Hall for the maps and to Emma Faull for the cover illustration.

S.U.

Introduction

A list of ancient authors who quote Herodotus or depend on him as a source would be very long, and the range of their subjects would be wide. The study of many areas of classical civilisation begins with him, for his interests include almost all aspects of the human and natural world as he found it on his travels. But to this insatiable appetite for information and knowledge Herodotus brought literary gifts which were remarkable in a prose author at this stage of the development of the medium. It was to the style and the artistic unity of his work that his ancient admirers pointed when they singled him out from a number of fifth-century prose writers and called him the Father of History. Some of his predecessors may have possessed talent for small-scale narrative, especially the Lydian Xanthus, from whom Herodotus may have drawn a taste for strange tales with an oriental flavour. Hecataeus of Miletus was certainly a discerning observer and a shrewd politician, whose geographical writings Herodotus used; and several other men, mainly Ionians, wrote local histories which survived to Augustan times. But it is clear from the words with which he begins his great work ('. . . to preserve the memory of the past by putting on record the astonishing achievements both of our own and of other peoples; and more particularly, to show why they came into conflict that Herodotus had a noble conception of his mighty subject, the struggle between the Greeks and the Barbarians, and that under his pen history would rival the older literary genres of epic, tragic and lyric poetry.

According to some of his ancient biographers Herodotus was a nephew or cousin of the epic poet Panyasis, who wrote of the exploits of Heracles. It is perhaps interesting that Herodotus was a member of a literary family , but his true literary ancestor was Homer, whose war was on a comparable scale of time and extent, who told of travels to strange places (in the *Odyssey*), and who recounted many episodes that divided his poem into parts which his audiences could enjoy in a number of separate sessions. Understanding the nature of Herodotus' audiences is the key to the understanding of much else. It is generally agreed that he read or recited sections of his history in the market-places of Athens

1

and other cities which he visited on his wide travels, and at Thurii
where he died. His audiences also listened to reciters of poetry
(*rhapsodes*) and attended productions of tragic and comic drama.
The popular idea that poets were divinely inspired must have
made the task of competing with them intimidating, especially in
prose and in a new genre. The beauty of his style made it seem that
Herodotus had somehow claimed some of the poets' inspiration
for himself, but he secured additional popularity from his audiences by stimulating their curiosity, sense of wonderment, patriotism, religion, and perhaps most of all, their interest in the
vicissitudes of human fortune. In providing the material for this
wide range of responses, his guiding principle was to tell all that he
had been told, leaving others to decide what was credible and what
was not: y business is to record what people say, but I am by no
means bound to believe it—and that may be taken to apply to this
book as a whole' (7.152.3). Behind this principle lies a respect for
tradition and mythology. He feels no licence to prune and edit his
sources, since such a procedure would both insult his audience's
intelligence and deprive them of entertainment. Stating his own
view on different versions of the same story, which he frequently
does, avoids both of these vices, while the general principle of
including all he has learnt has placed later historians deeply in his
debt and made his history a veritable storehouse of historical
information covering periods well outside the time of his main
subject.

Herodotus not only tells us all he has discovered, but does so in
the main without personal bias. Opinions of actions and motives
are mostly ascribed to the participants themselves, and delivered
in live speech. Though he shares his fellow-countrymen's satisfaction at the outcome of the war, he says much which implies
admiration of the Persian Empire and criticism of the Greeks. The
main issue between them is their different way of life: the Persians
(and other barbarians) prefer to live in slavery under an absolute
monarch, and consider this a natural condition for the human race;
the Greeks incline to freedom under the rule of law, and will
defend it regardless of the cost. The Persian way leads to an
unending quest for dominion, and Herodotus' *History* traces this
quest from its beginning to its catastrophic end. The division of the
work into nine books was made by a later librarian, but it accords
well with the overall plan of the narrative, which is tripartite. The
first three books tell of the rise of Persia under its greatest king
Cyrus and his successors. Books 4–6 tell how the wider ambitions
of Darius I are thwarted and Greece becomes involved with him

through the Ionian Revolt. Books 7–9 contain the climax, both historical and artistic, to the story, with Book 7 the most important because it is the book of decision, in which the central figure, King Xerxes, deliberates and finally decides to embark upon the fateful expedition after weighing all advice and wrestling with his own character and emotions. In this book are concentrated most of the ingredients that set Herodotus apart from his predecessors. Themes which have hitherto been the preserve of the poets now find their place in the actions, thoughts and words of historical characters, and in the historian's interpretation of them. To some of these we shall return.

His conception of his work as an 'enquiry' (*historiê*) meant that his chief task prior to its composition was to seek information. The sources available to him were varied in both nature and reliability. His ignorance of foreign languages put him at a disadvantage in dealing with Persian and Egyptian affairs, so that in these areas he was often at the mercy of an interpreter, who could be an extra source of distortion. Even in Greek-speaking environments little documentary evidence was available to him, and not much relevant historical writing apart from that of Hecataeus. Furthermore, he had few opportunities to collect evidence at first hand, since most of the events he narrates occurred during his infancy and before. His sole remaining source was the conversation he held with the men he met on his travels, and it was this oral tradition that furnished him with by far the largest part of his information. Most of his informants were probably men of some importance in their several cities, and priests and other religious officials may have given him access to temple records. In cities where he resided for some time, like Athens, he would have had long conversations with jmembers of the aristocratic families, and he mixed generally in the upper circles of society. Consequently he tended to express the views of the governing class 'establishment view' of events,(though he did not åalways do so uncritically), and to cut himself off from sources which might have given him a broader view of events and their causes.

This dependence on mainly aristocratic sources had further consequences. One of the most important of these is the prominence he gives to the careers of individuals, to the exclusion of popular opinions and a balanced estimate of the effects of events upon ordinary people. An example of this is the lack of consideration given to the positive benefits conferred by some tyrants upon their cities, an omission explained by the fact that tyrannies were generally hated by the aristocracy and often popular among the rest of the citizens, especially during their early reforming stages. His account of the Ionian revolt dwells exclusively upon the careers of Aristagoras and Histiaeus, while the territorial ambitions of Croesus, Cyrus, Cambyses and Darius are given as the only causes of the westward expansion of the barbarian empires. Dealing in personalities, careers, aspirations and mistakes, Herodotus drew on a moralising literary tradition already firmly established in tragic and lyric poetry. A moralistic mode of thought colours many of his stories: excessive exploitation of power or wealth leads to disaster, and too much success is bad for a man because it provokes envy, both human and divine. The quest for happiness is to be made not through material acquisitions but by leading an exemplary life and observing the customs of your society. Belief in these moral concepts sometimes leads to fatalism when they are perceived to have been neglected: if a project fails, it is because it was ill-conceived and doomed from the start because of a moral flaw in its author.

This mode of thought is rooted in religion, since the ultimate dispensers of justice, punishers of evil and exactors of revenge are the gods. Herodotus' priestly sources were probably not only responsible for such stories as that of the Persian army's approach to Delphi (8.35–39) and the many oracular pronouncements he records, but also influenced his attitude to them. He tells stories of divine intervention and observes the fulfilment of oracles with a degree of satisfaction which seems to suggest personal belief rather than the mere paying of lip service to the popular religion of his time. At the same time, however, the responsibility which he imposes on men for their own errors is clearly defined: they must not expect the gods to assist their plans if they are unreasonable (8.60.c). Reason also plays its part in establishing the role of religion in Herodotus' narrative as a whole. People believe that the gods play a part in human affairs; therefore their actions often need to be explained by reference to this belief, and the activities and pronouncements of the gods, whether supposed or imaginary, must be recorded as an integral part of the human story. Herodotus shows no devotion to particular gods, and freely discusses comparative religion (1.131). In his story the gods are chiefly agents of vengeance, and they are on the Greek side (8.13). Other more abstract agencies were Chance (*tuchê*, so important in the later historian Polybius, who was nevertheless one of the most scientific of the ancient historians); and Fate (*moira*), one of whose functions is to distribute prosperity so that no individual receives more than his share (*meros*). The instability of human fortune is a recurrent theme in the *History*, while the gods intervene on particular occasions when their authority is challenged or their interests threatened. Finally, dreams, omens and portents find their natural place in a narrative which truly tells all that people heard and saw, and all that influenced them in their actions.

An even more direct and powerful influence on people's actions was exerted by their own and others' reasoning and argument. But how were these to be presented to audiences and readers ? Herodotus needed only to refer to his mentor Homer to realise that the inclusion of live speech transformed a narrative into a drama and enabled the writer to give greater scope to his literary talents. Most of the speeches in Herodotus are free literary compositions, since he could not have known what was actually said. One of their chief functions is to supply an understanding of general motivation, and another is to portray individual character; while the vividness and variety which they confer upon the narrative are priceless literary assets. It is easy to imagine that some of the historical characters whose souls are laid bare by Herodotus through their utterances (significantly, more Persian leaders come to mind than Greeks), made a profounder impression on the minds of his listeners than many of the heroic figures portrayed in tragic drama, whose presentation was restricted by the dramatic rules of time and stage convention. Herodotus took full advantage of the freedom of the new literary form of history: the epic sweep of his subject was very much to his taste, as was the scope it afforded for division into many episodes and digressions. But in spite of the work's vast scale, its unity is clearly discernible: within a complex framework in which contacts between the Greek and barbarian world serve only to bring out their differences, movement towards the final conflict is inexorable, and its outcome frequently foreshadowed. His readers knew it, but his retelling of the story was also a re-creation of dramatic situations and heroic characters, a travelogue describing strange places and customs, ιand an occasional excursion into matters of scientific, political and philosophical interest. Something, in fact, for every thinking person to ponder. Hence its universal popularity, which so annoyed some of his more 'serious' successors; and therein, no less, its charm.

The races of the Medes and Persians and their royal houses were closely related, and their union under Cyrus the Great around the middle of the sixth century B.C. created a coherent new nation which combined military strength with wealth and dynamic leadership. The opportunity to exploit these assets came when her western neighbour, King Croesus of Lydia, perhaps hoping to take advantage of the confusion attending the reorganisation of the nascent kingdom, launched an invasion. Famous for the wealth which the invention of coinage and thriving trade connections had brought him, Croesus had conquered the Ionian Greeks but had himself become partly hellenised as the two civilisations came under one another's influence. He paid court to the Greek gods and adorned their temples. But he failed to understand the enigmatic nature of their oracles, so that when he consulted Apollo at Delphi concerning his projected invasion of Persia, and the oracle predicted that he would estroy a mighty kingdom he mistook a hedged bet for a direct invitation. Cyrus was at the gates of his capital city ,of Sardis in less than a year (546). The fate of Croesus is described by Herodotus (1.86–92). The effective result of his vain ambition was that his Greek subjects came under Cyrus' rule along with the rest of his empire.

Exchanging the rule of Croesus for that of Cyrus was a painful experience for the Ionians. Some of them had fought for Croesus in spite of Cyrus' invitation to join his side. The new regime was more systematically oppressive than the old, with regular taxes exacted by local representatives of the now remote conqueror, who returned eastward to conquer Babylon and extend his empire into Afghanistan. On Cyrus' death his son Cambyses conquered the ancient kingdom of Egypt (526–522). He died in Syria while returning to crush a rebellion led by a usurper, the false Smerdis, but the Achaemenid succession was re-established when Darius came to the throne in 521 and married Atossa, daughter of Cyrus. It was Darius who reorganised the empire, now at its greatest extent, and reminded the Ionian Greeks of their subject status by reimposing fixed taxes after a period of laxity (c.518). In 512 B.C. he made his first expedition into Europe, striking north to the Danube and the Ukraine beyond. In the course of this expedition, and particularly during his hazardous return, he received vital naval and engineering support from the Ionian Greeks. After his withdrawal, he left an army in Europe under his general Megabazus, who conquered Thrace as far west as the river Strymon and induced the Macedonians to recognize Darius as their overlord. The Great King's western policy at this stage, if he had one, seems to have been opportunistic rather than systematic. He would have liked to establish in Greek cities puppet tyrants on the Ionian model, and his satrap Artaphernes tried to persuade the Athenians to take back their deposed tyrant Hippias, son of Pisistratus. They refused; but more blatant defiance of the King's power was needed to precipitate direct conflict. This came with the Ionian Revolt, the point at which we join Herodotus' *History*.

Commentary

5.28–38: Ionian Revolt: the Beginning

Some indication of the likely limitations of Herodotus' account of the Ionian Revolt is to be found in the preceding chapters. In these, as in the narrative of the revolt itself, his only informants seem either to have had connections in the Persian court or more or less close contacts among the ruling families in some of the Ionian cities. An unhappy consequence of this is his inability to throw direct light on two related questions of central importance: was there a general revolutionary movement in Ionia at this time (around 5OO B.C.), and, if so, what was its cause? His concentration upon the careers of individual leaders tends to obstruct any attempts to arrive at clear answers to these questions, but because of Herodotus' admirable policy of telling all he knows about a wide range of events throughout the Greek world, the search for them within his pages, aided by inference, is by no means futile. Ionian trade had been widely disrupted by the Persian conquests, especially that of Egypt and the southern coast of the Black Sea. In these straitened circumstances, the burden of tribute, which was already high by comparison with that levied under the later Athenian empire, must have seemed increasingly oppressive. Finally, the subject-status which its payment symbolised contrasted starkly with the political changes that had recently taken place in Greece, especially the Ionians' mother-city Athens, whence the tyrant Hippias had been expelled and where the reforms of Cleisthenes had established a peculiarly pure form of democracy. Herodotus was fully aware of the democratic aspirations of the Ionians (4.137.3). When the Naxian expedition was mounted and a united Ionian naval force assembled under Persian command, nationalist feeling was aroused; and this was stimulated further by the clash between the Persian and Ionian leadership which Herodotus describes. Careful reading and analysis of his wide-ranging narrative of events throughout the Greek world, including Southern Italy, where the destruction of Sybaris (5.44; 6.21) which had close connections with Miletus, may have had an indirect bearing on events in Ionia (see next note), provide the material for numerous theories as to the origins of the revolt. Its occurrence

9

becomes more baffling with each new study. In one of the most recent, H.T. Wallinga, 'The Ionian Revolt', *Mnemosyne* 37 (1984) 417ff. argues that the presence of the Persian navy in the Aegean was acceptable to some Greeks as a protection against Samian piracy.

28.1. Then trouble ceased for a while: The viewpoint is Persian, following on from the previous chapter. **Naxos and Miletus:** Naxos flourished under the tyranny of Lygdamis, but his deposition around 520 led to a period of political turmoil. Miletus was prosperous throughout the 6th century, but may have gone through a difficult phase at the end of that century following the destruction of Sybaris (510 B.C.), her richest trading partner, wool being one of the major items of commerce. Thus both these Ionian states were subject to unsettling influences at this time, Naxos for mainly political and Miletus for mainly economic reasons.

29. The story of the Parian arbitration would be more enlightening if it could be dated with some precision. **Previously** (28) could indicate a period in the 6th century between the tyranny of Thrasybulus and that of Histiaeus. The constitution which the Parians chose for Miletus was apparently oligarchic (**the men whose land they found in good order**). The rule of these oligarchs ended when Histiaeus was appointed by Darius, following his usual practice of ruling the Ionian states through puppet tyrants. The origin and nature of Histiaeus' rule is clearly described in 4.137 (p.287), where Herodotus tells how motives of self-preservation caused him to prevent the abandonment of the bridge over the Danube which would probably have led to the death of Darius. For the view of Histiaeus as the loyal servant of Darius, see A. Blamire, *Classical Quarterly* 9 (1959), 142–154, arguing primarily against G.B. Grundy, *The Great Persian War and its Preliminaries* (London, 1901) 141.

30.1. Certain substantial citizens of Naxos (lit. 'fat', like colloqu. American 'fat cats'): the oligarchic successors of the tyrant Lygdamis.

30.2. Aristagoras, nominated by Histiaeus as his temporary regent at Miletus, was eager to pursue ambitions of his own. The attraction of Naxos was not only its wealth, but also the fact that it was an island not yet subjected to Persia. It is credible that Aristagoras could have believed that the Persians, after supplying him with the armed forces to enable him to establish his rule, would leave him to continue it without undue interference, since that was their policy both with their Ionian puppets and their own satraps. For practical purposes of administration Persian provincial government was decentralised. Credible also are the arguments with which Herodotus makes Aristagoras fire the enthusiasm of the satrap Artaphernes and Darius (31–32) (though Herodotus cannot of course have known what was actually said, and creates his own dialogue here as elsewhere). Darius' expedition to Scythia and the Danube afforded proof of his policy of expanding his empire in any direction where prospects of conquest seemed good.

33–34. This part of the story bristles with improbabilities. It seems highly unlikely that Megabates would have risked the wrath of Darius by causing the failure of a plan which the King had approved. His alleged treachery must therefore be discounted as an Ionian tale attempting to explain the preparedness of the Naxians, which doomed the expedition. Its outcome was perhaps less important than its preliminaries in relation to the Revolt: disaffection in the fleet, with Persian officers disciplining Ionian sailors, gave rise to nationalist feelings. For this view, see J.A.S. Evans, *American Journal of Philology* 84 (1963) 118–121.

35–36. Further difficulties arise from H's account of subsequent events. Aristagoras was clearly in an embarrassing position, but the arrival of Histiaeus' message, and his reason for sending it (**distress at being detained in Susa**) (35.4), serve only to enhance, and also to confuse, the personal motivation. The message itself is puzzling. Did Histiaeus simply tattoo the word *apostasis* on his slave's head? Surely such a momentous command required some explanation, unless it was perhaps a prearranged signal which Aristagoras would understand; in which case Herodotus should have explained the circumstances. Did Histiaeus, from three thousand miles away, judge that the time was ripe for rebellion? How was he able to judge the chances of success? It is at this point in the story (36.1) that Herodotus reveals, incidentally, the first evidence of a revolutionary movement, or rather a group of citizens who had been contemplating rebellion. He calls them *hoi stasitai*,which could mean merely 'supporters' as De Selincourt translates, but the word usually implies membership of a faction dedicated to some political aim (N.B. when he describes Aristagoras' supporters later (5.124.2) he calls them *sustasiôtai*). Their swift agreement to revolt would thus be explained. But Herodotus, whose views on the Revolt were coloured by its outcome (cf.33.2 **the Naxians were not destined** . . . for a similar example of determinism), concentrates on the arguments of the sole dissenter. **The historian Hecataeus** is one of the best-informed of the tragic warners in Herodotus, who used his material extensively, especially for his account of Egypt in Book 2. Often critical of the earlier historian, Herodotus takes this opportunity to show his respect for his pioneering predecessor (See Penguin Introd. pp. 24–5). Hecataeus' lone dissenting voice was the expression of a sceptical and scientific mind, reminding the reader that Miletus was the home of the first Greek philosophical thinkers. But politics may also have been involved in Hecataeus' thinking. It is likely that he saw the ambitions of Aristagoras as an interruption to long-term plans for a Hellenic thalassocracy (sea-empire) centred on Miletus, which had been under discussion in the city for some time. When he saw that his colleagues were intent on rebellion, he proposed accelerating the implementation of those plans by enlarging the fleet and gaining command of the sea. By **the weakness of Miletus** (36.3) H means weakness in comparison to the vast resources of the Persian empire, since he says earlier (28) that Miletus, like Naxos, was **at the peak of her prosperity**. The **long list of the nations under Persian dominion** would be derived from Hecataeus' *Genealogies*, his major geographical work.

36.4. the fleet's commanders were also tyrants of their respective cities. The deposition of these puppets of Persia was a logical and necessary preliminary to rebellion. Aristagoras' payment of lip-service to **democratic government** suggests one of the many changes aimed at by the *stasiôtai* (4.137.3), who were inspired by the democratic movements in Athens, Argos and most recently on Naxos.

38.2. Aristagoras' hopes of success in his **mission to Lacedaemon** rested on the current belief that Sparta was the most powerful state in Greece, and also that her leaders would offer protection to oppressed Greeks well beyond her own immediate sphere of interest, the Peloponnese. Reasons for the second of these beliefs may be traced to the time of Cyrus the Great's conquest of Ionia, when appeals to Sparta drew a stern rebuke for the Persian, though no physical aid for the Ionians (1.152.3). They had also invaded Samos to dislodge the tyrant Polycrates (3.39, 44–56). Scholars have been too ready to reject these examples of positive Spartan policy towards Ionia, citing their withdrawal after the Persian War, which took place after a costly conflict and in embarrassment at the behaviour of their king Pausanias (Thuc. 1.95.7).

5.49–51

49.1. Aristagoras' **map of the world** was based on the specula-
tions of Anaximander and later Hecataeus, who envisaged the
world as flat and circular, surrounded by Ocean. Some Ionian
maps were ridiculed by H (4.36.2). See J.O. Thomson, *History of
Ancient Geography* (Cambridge, 1948) 97–99. The argument
propounded by Aristagoras would have appeared preposterous to
most Greeks even after the victories in 479 B.C. Indeed, the
ethnological excursus might be expected to have had the opposite
effect to that desired. What seems to have happened is that H,
having introduced the subject of maps, naturally proceeds to
describe the regions depicted on them. The promise of untold
wealth from strange foreign places gives the story an exotic eastern
flavour, but historically it is anachronistic.

5.97–125 : Ionian Revolt: Hostilities
H returns to his narrative of the Ionian Revolt after recounting the
last years of the Pisistratid tyranny at Athens, to which he appends
material illustrative of the worst excesses of tyranny. The readiness of the Athenians to assist is explained by their hostility against
Persia for trying to restore the expelled tyrant Hippias. This
enables Herodotus to excuse them for aiding a doomed cause: they
were **already on bad terms with Persia** (97.1). As to H's own
attitude to tyranny, he preferred to form his judgement according
to the effectiveness of each individual ruler rather than to general-
ise on vague moral criteria. See K.H. Walters, *Herodotus the
Historian* (London, 1985) 131–132. He was thoroughly conversant
with the current arguments for and against the three recognised
forms of government—monarchy, oligarchy and democracy. In
the famous debate of the Persian leaders following the death of
Cambyses (3.80–82), the most vehement criticism is reserved for
the 'mob', and H's strictures here on the gullibility of the **thirty
thousand Athenians** probably reflect his own views on the weak-
nesses of democracy. As in the above discussion, leadership is the
crucial factor: H's Athenian aristocratic friends would have
wholeheartedly agreed, as would have Thucydides (2.65.8–9).
Thirty thousand is the conventional figure for the adult male
population of Athens in the 5th century, but not more than six
thousand of these could have heard Aristagoras addressing the
Popular Assembly.

97.3. **Beginning** **of** **trouble** (pref. 'evils'): A
portentous and pessimistic pronouncement, with a poetic ring

(cf. Homer *Iliad* 5.62; 11.604; see also Thuc. 2.12). H refuses to applaud a bid for freedom which is destined to fail.

98–102. The early stages of the revolt, in which the Athenians and Eretrians were involved, are described in such a way as to emphasise that they conducted their part of the campaign competently enough; but Aristagoras began by adopting **a plan of action from which no advantage could possibly accrue to the Ionians** (98.1), and **did not himself accompany the expedition** (99.2) against Sardis , which was led on the Ionian side without the resolve necessary to press home their initial success and ended in defeat at Ephesus.

99.1. The Eretrians' **war with the Chalcidians** over the Lelantine Plain was traditionally regarded as the first pan-Hellenic war, and belongs to the 7th century (see Thuc. 1.15.3). Its origin was probably commercial, hence the involvement of the Western Greek cities of Sybaris and Croton on opposing sides.

102.1. temple of Cybebe . . . was destroyed . . . pretext: H's narrative suggests that the burning of this temple was accidental; and indeed the Ionians had no rational motive for dishonouring a Lydian deity whose cult later attracted Greek adherents, and closely resembled that of the Hellenic Great Mother goddess. The Persians would probably have regarded Cybebe as a deity no less foreign than the Greek pantheon; hence the hollowness of their 'pretext' (cf. 6.101.3; 7.8,b 3). The Ionian march on Sardis, difficult to explain strategically in isolation, may have been a counter-attack to the Persian assault on Miletus (Plutarch, *On the Malice of Herodotus* 24, quoting Lysanias of Mallos).

103–4. The spread of the revolt is described in a few rapid sentences, with no reference to Ionian leadership or a concerted plan. H's interests lie elsewhere—in resuming the career of Histiaeus from 5.36 and the story of Darius' concern at the intervention of the Athenians.

105. Darius . . . .did not give a thought to the Ionians, sharing the contempt felt for them by his predecessor Cyrus (1.153). Following his brief description of the spread of the revolt, H's addition of this disparaging note confirms his own prejudices. But the main theme, summarised in the words **remember the Athenians**, is important from a literary point of view, as illustrating the arrogance and ignorance of an oriental potentate, who is obsessed with his own power, and 'punishes' those who oppose it. It is interesting that, in the *Persians* of Aeschylus, the ghost of Darius warns his family against *hybris*, and urges them to 'remember the Athenians and Greece' (825). It seems likely that Aeschylus adapted the well-known story of which H gives the original version. The importance of the story from a historical viewpoint is no less great, embodying an idea of historical destiny which would have appealed to his Athenian readers.

109.1. the city-chief of Cyprus seems to have differed in status from the Ionian puppet-tyrants. His island afforded him greater autonomy and less regular Persian supervision: hence perhaps the readiness with which he joined Onesilus in rebelling. But the effect of this whole action was to weaken the main effort by diverting Ionian forces from the central theatre of war.

109.3. The common council of Ionia: The *Panionion* met as a deliberat- ive body when originally threatened by Cyrus (1.141). Prior to that its functions had been mainly cultural and religious (1.141–151). While wishing to confirm their racial identity, the Ionians rejected proposals designed to effect political unity (1.170). See M.O.B. Caspari, 'The Ionian League', *Journal of Hellenic Studies* 35 (1915) 173–188; C. Roebuck, 'The Early Ionian League', *Classical Philology* 50 (1955) 26–40.

114.1. The head of Onesilus . . . swarm of bees: Bees figured in religious observance, notably in the cult of Artemis. They appear on Ephesian coins, and a college of priests there were called the King Bees (Pausanias 8.13.1).

116.1. after a year of freedom: The actual fighting had lasted about seven months, from summer 497 to winter 497/6. H's narrative now reads like a series of desultory mopping-up opera- tions, beginning with the Hellespontine cities, captured (117) in order to clear the way for an advance from the south-west to the north-east. Indications of chronology, which would probably have given a truer picture of the seriousness of the uprising and the difficulty of suppressing it, are entirely absent. H has rather more details of events in Caria, where he had personal connections. The Carians had had time to prepare, but were overwhelmed by weight of numbers (Autumn 496).

125–126. However satisfying Aristagoras' end may have seemed to H from a moral point of view, he has given him too much prominence and responsiblity. His combination of facile plausibility, selfish adventurism and ultimate cowardice personal- ises for H the conception of the whole affair. Yet it took Darius five years to suppress the revolt. Again, his relationship with Histiaeus is sufficiently unclear to have given rise to much specula- tion. G.A.H. Chapman, 'Herodotus and Histiaeus' Role in the Ionian Revolt', *Historia* 21 (1972) 546–568, regards Histiaeus as ultimately responsible for the revolt; while P.B. Manville,

'Aristagoras and Histiaios: the Leadership Struggle in the Ionian Revolt', *Classical Quarterly* 27 (1977) 80, argues that the revolt arose from a power-struggle between the two Milesians. On balance scholars have tended to blame Histiaeus, since he remained nominally ruler of Miletus, with Aristagoras his regent. In 5.106 Darius calls upon him to account for the behaviour of his deputy (*epitropos*).

6.1–21: Ionian Revolt: the End

2.1. Artaphernes knew the truth: H thus endorses the satrap's opinion. Histiaeus' **real purpose** in starting the revolt was his desire to return to Miletus from Susa (5.35).

4.1. Persians in Sardis: These seem to have been intriguing against Artaphernes, encouraged by Histiaeus, though with what long-term objective it is difficult to imagine, However, their existence is a good indication of the chances of success which the revolt was thought to have, even by the Persians.

5. Chios was a natural refuge for a Milesian leader, as the two states had long been on close terms. But the democratic movement had spread to Chios, and the Chians refused to back Histiaeus against the wishes of the people of Miletus. His story is resumed in 26 and ends in 30.

7. the Panionium . . . decided to raise no troops: Confirming that there was effective central command (see 5.109). The expulsion of the puppet-tyrants must have increased the power of this council. No doubt the Milesians, on the advice of Hecataeus, were among the strongest advocates of a naval campaign, and they would have been strongly backed by the Chians. By contrast, there was apparently no great enthusiasm for mounting a land campaign against the immensely superior Persian military machine, and indeed no tradition of hoplite fighting among the Ionians.

8. the Ionian fleet: The absence of Dorian states such as H's own city of Halicarnassus and the Rhodian cities shows the limits of the revolt. But the purely Ionian composition of the fleet made it a more integrated unit than the combined fleets of Phoenicia, Cyprus and Egypt. These may have outnumbered the Ionian ships, but the figure of 600 is suspiciously conventional (cf. Artemisium and Salamis below). The Ionians were not only pioneers among the Greeks in naval warfare, but their combined strength (about half of which was supplied by Miletus and Chios) more then matched that of other Greek states until Syracuse and Athens built navies around 480.

10. firmly refused the invitation to treachery: Rather 'showed obstinacy', which does H less credit and suggests perhaps a Samian source, excusing the behaviour of their contingent in the battle.

11.1. The Phocaean commander Dionysius: The Phocaeans founded the colony of Massilia (mod. Marseilles) and were among the most enterprising of Greek navigators. Also, their devotion to freedom was undoubted, since they had chosen to emigrate rather than accept Persian rule; though some became homesick and returned (1.163–167). The reduced size of their state accounts for their inability to furnish a fleet to match their past reputation, but the expertise of their commander was recognised.

11.2. balances on a razor's edge: Probably a popular metaphor derived from Homer (*Iliad* 10.173). H's version of Dionysius' speech presupposes that the Ionians sorely needed a disciplinarian commander.

12.1 'breaking the line': This manoeuvre required precise co-ordination and seamanship of a high order. It involved gathering enough momentum to sail through the enemy line, shipping or retracting oars while doing so and fouling the enemy oars and rudder, sometimes sailing round (*periplous*) and ramming him astern. See also 8.9n. and J.S. Morrison and R.T. Williams, *Greek Oared Ships* (Cambridge, 1968) 137–139.

12.4. refused . . . training . . . : The significance of this carica-ture of Ionian indiscipline becomes apparent when H switches quickly to the Samians, (13) whose desertion at the height of the battle could not be denied or ignored. His decision to follow a Samian source, which causes him to distance 'the Samians' from 'the Ionians', not only squares with his overall view of the revolt, but enables him both to gratify both his Samian friends and the Athenians, who liked to compare Lade with the triumph at Salamis. On H's Samian connections, see B.M. Mitchell, 'Hero-dotus and Samos', *Journal of Hellenic Studies* 95 (1975) 75–91; and on this passage, see D. Lateiner, 'The Failure of the Ionian Revolt', *Historia* 31 (1982) 151–157.

14.1. I cannot say for certain: Naval battles involving large fleets were notoriously difficult to observe, especially by the combatants themselves, who only saw their own part of the action and exaggerated their own exploits. Spectators were little better placed (Thuc. 7.71.3). H faced a similar problem with Salamis, and is equally candid (8.87.1).

15–16. The sad end of the Chians at the hands of the Ephesians seems to require a different explanation from that given by H, who appears to believe that the Ephesians did not know about the battle at Lade. Their behaviour suggests that, after staying aloof from the earlier fighting, they acted in the Persian interest when they saw the Ionian cause was lost.

17. The subsequent career of Dionysius of Phocaea, the sole personality to emerge from the battle of Lade, would have elicited the same sort of approval from H's readers as the later career of Sir Francis Drake won from readers of Elizabethan history: selective patriotic piracy was considered respectable in both ages.

18. five years: For the chronology of the revolt, see N.G.L. Hammond, 'Studies in Greek Chronology in the Sixth and Fifth Centuries B.C.', *Historia* 4 (1955) 385–411. The revolt had started when Aristagoras expelled the tyrants from Ionian cities in 499 (5.37). Although other dates are controversial, the capture of Miletus can be confidently assigned to 494.

19. The linking of Miletus with Argos may have arisen through the visit to Greece of Aristagoras, who may have asked the Argives for help after his rejection at Sparta. The Argives, before considering his request, sought assurance from the Delphic oracle that they were not themselves in danger of attack, probably from Sparta. Delphi, having already formed the opinion that Persia was unconquerable, advised the Argives against having anything to do with Aristagoras, and concluded the audience by prophesying disaster for his venture and his city. Whether Miletus was **emptied of its inhabitants** may be doubted, since Milesians were present at the Mycale campaign in 479 (9.104).

21.2. The innovation of basing a drama upon an historical event, the emotive character of that event, and the prominence of musical and choreographic elements in the drama of this early period all combined to exert an overwhelming effect upon the Athenian audience. Phrynichus later (476) celebrated the victories over Persia in his *Phoenissae*.

For further study of H's treatment of the Ionian revolt, see P. Tozzi, *La Rivolta Ionica* (Pisa, 1978); M. Lang, 'Herodotus and the Ionian Revolt', *Historia* 17 (1968) 24–36; K.H. Waters, 'Herodotos and the Ionian Revolt', *Historia* 19 (1970) 504–508.

6.94–136: The Marathon Campaign

94.1. Athens and Aegina: Probably not a single full-scale conflict, but desultory and intermittent hostilities, such that they were not considered dangerous enough to prevent a major expedition from going to Paros in 489, but could still be adduced by Themistocles in 483 as a reason for building a large Athenian fleet.

The Pisistratidae and their intrigues were the main reason for the resentment against Persia that led the Athenians to assist the Ionians (5.97n). It is even possible that the withdrawal of Athenian support during the revolt itself was the result of a change of policy following the appointment as archon of Hipparchus, a member of the tyrant's family. Hippias was still confident that he could attract support in Athens.

to conquer all the Greek communities which refused to give earth and water: Darius' immediate purpose was to punish Athens and Eretria, but H is right to assert that he also aimed to secure any territory he could in the course of his advance, if only for strategic reasons. The recent campaign of Mardonius (see below) and his own to Scythia vividly illustrated the dangers of expeditions into Europe, and warned Darius to pursue his objectives in that continent with caution. But Athens and Eretria seemed to offer good chances of securing a foothold. Conquest of these cities could be followed by the installation of puppet tyrants (ready at hand in the case of Athens) supported by Persian garrisons. Then it was a matter of waiting for the next opportunity.

94.2. previous expedition ... Mardonius: See 6.43–45. This was really the first expedition against Athens and Eretria, but as in the last passage, H says (44.1) that the Persians intended to conquer as many Greek cities as they could. His brief account shows that he lacked detailed information about this expedition, which is hardly surprising.

Datis ... Artaphernes: Datis was the senior commander: Artaphernes, son of the satrap of Sardis, who was a brother of Darius, was inexperienced and probably young at this time.

95.1. horse-transports ... tributary states the year before: See 48. The tributary states now included the Ionians. The following reference to the transport of horses on warships is the earliest we have.

95.2. The fleet sailed westward along the south coast of Turkey and hugged that coast northward as far as Samos. Being thus an entirely sea-borne expedition, its numbers were restricted; and once again (see 6.8n) **six hundred vessels** is probably a conventional overestimate.

Naxos ... the first objective of the war: Hence dread of the passage round Athos was not the main reason for choosing the route through the Cyclades. To the cautious Darius, a naval advance called for the same attention to lines of communication as an advance over land. He had no reason to expect strong naval opposition from the Greeks, but the whole procedure was novel,

and the Cyclades were needed to provide harbourage. The treatment of the islanders as described by H suggests that the Persians
intended permanent occupation of the Cyclades; but he had
literary reasons for calling attention to the Persian excesses, both
in order to contrast them with Datis' behaviour on Delos (97) and
to complete the cycle of *hybris-nemesis* with the Athenian victory
at Marathon.

97.1. Delos afforded Datis an opportunity to indulge in some
timely propaganda. Whereas the Naxians, like the Athenians and
Eretrians, had defied the King and thereby invited his vengeance,
the Delians were neutral and inhabited a sacred island. Other
Greek states which gave no offence might hope for similar
indulgence. To be seen showing respect for one of the major
centres of Ionian culture was potentially advantageous. There is
no need to suppose that Datis' treatment of Delos was the result of
advice from Hippias, as suggested by How & Wells and Macan.
His conciliatory act may be taken at face-value.

98.1. It may well be that the shock was an act of God: H follows
his usual rational approach to supernatural phenomena and their
bearing upon events. Disaster actually followed the earthquakes,
therefore they *may* have portended it. His attitude to oracles is
similar: since they are seen accurately to forecast events, their
predictions should be taken seriously (see 8.77n).

99.1. Carystus had good harbourage and abundant water, and
afforded a good base for operations against both Athens and
Eretria. H seems to sympathise with the Carystians' plight both
here and in 8.112, when Themistocles extorts money from them;
and when he numbers Carystians among those who contribute
reinforcements to Xerxes' fleet (8.66), he merely lists them with
others in a catalogue intended to magnify the Persian forces before
Salamis. Evidently they valued their independence to an unusual
degree (9.105; Thuc.1.98), and the charge of medism was morally
unjustified. As Macan says: 'The conduct of the Karystians is in
strong contrast to that of the Ionians and Aeolians.'

100.1. The Athenians brought no effective aid to Eretria. H
preserves the tradition that exonerates them: **things at Eretria
were not in a healthy state.** Yet in the event the Eretrians fought
with commendable resolve. If **counsels were divided** before the
enemy assault on their city, they appear to have settled their
differences in time to present a united front against overwhelm-
ingly superior odds. The betrayal of the city by two traitors
probably reflects the true state of affairs in Eretria. But if strategic
considerations were to dictate their course of action, the Athenians

needed no justification for abandoning Eretria. Two factors determined their strategy: the enemy's superior numbers and the
mobility conferred on him by his control of the sea. If they sent the
major part of their forces to defend Eretria, the Persian fleet,
equipped for the purpose (95.1), could transport a large detachment of the army, including cavalry, to Athens, now undefended,
while still outnumbering the combined forces of Athens and
Eretria at Eretria.

**102. The part of Attic territory nearest Eretria—and also the best
ground for cavalry to manouevre in . . . Hippias directed the
invading army**: The Persian choice of Marathon was both political
and strategic. Hippias had returned this way with his father
Pisistratus (540/539), also from Eretria, gathering support from
this district of Attica. Toi Datis, the prospect of an unopposed
landing and time to organise his forces was attractive. The
suitability of the terrain for cavalry may have been a secondary
consideration, defensive in conception from the Persian point of
view in that it rendered an initial assault by the Athenians unlikely
and placed all the tactical options in Datis' hands. The fact that the
Persian cavalry was never engaged at Marathon has been variously
explained. The best explanation may be that the Athenians
launched their attack when the Persians, having waited for ten
days, were in the process of embarkation, for which the animals
would have to be put on board first. See A.W. Gomme, 'Herodotus and Marathon', *Phoenix* 6 (1952) 82–83. G. Shrimpton,
'Persian Cavalry at Marathon', *Phoenix* 34 (1980) 20–37 argues
that the Persian cavalry was initially present, but fled during the
battle. See also N.G.L. Hammond, 'The Campaign and Battle of
Marathon', *Journal of Hellenic Studies* 88 (1968) 13–57 and
criticisms by A.R. Burn in *Journal of Hellenic Studies* 89 (1969)
118–119.

103.1: of whom the tenth was Miltiades : By thus focussing
attention on Miltiades H prepares us for the vital part he plays
later (109ff.).

104.2. elected a general by the people: Note the indefinite article:
he was appointed to the generalship over his own tribe, which
nominally conferred equal power with the other nine generals,
who each led their own tribes. The official overall commander was
the War Archon (*Polemarch*), Callimachus.

105.1. The name **Pheidippides** ('son of the sparer of horses') is
suspicious, and 'Philippides', found in other ancient sources
(Pausanias 1.28.4; 8.54.6; Plut. *On the Malice of Herodotus* 26), is
probably to be preferred. But see E. Badian, 'The Name of the

Runner', *American Journal of Ancient History* 4 (1979) 163–166.
The length of the modern Marathon race is the distance of
Marathon from Athens (26 miles). It originated from a later story
that Philippides joined the Athenian army at Marathon and died
after bringing the news of the Athenian victory to Athens. The
Athenian appeal to Sparta was prompted by recent Spartan
actions and policies. They had warned the Persians against inter-
fering in Greek affairs (1.152.3) and expelled Hippias from Athens
(5.65).

106.3. The Spartans' refusal to **take the field until the moon was
full** evokes no criticism from H, which is hardly surprising in view
of his own strong religiosity. Moreover, their action has many
historical parallels, of which one of the most notorious was Nicias'
refusal to allow the Athenian fleet to sail away from Sicily in 413
after an eclipse of the moon. Thucydides saw this as an act of folly
(7.50.4). The more religiously conventional Xenophon, on the
other hand, takes pleasure in recounting many instances of religious observance before battles and at the outset of campaigns,
especially by the Spartan king Agesilaus.

**107.1. Hippias had dreamed that he was sleeping with his
mother**: For the identification of a mother-figure in dreams with
one's native country, cf. Suetonius, *Divus Julius* 7.

107.3. sneezing was itself thought to be a divine portent, which
could be turned to advantage by a timely prayer (Xen. *Anab.*
3.2.9). The loss of a tooth, however, was always a bad omen.

**108.3. the Spartans' desire to embroil Athens in quarrels with the
Boeotians** in 519/8, the date of the Athens/Plataea alliance (Thuc.
3.68), is perhaps to be explained as an example of an unchanging
Spartan policy of trying to perpetuate her own supremacy by
either setting her strongest neighbours against one another, as in
this case, or by maintaining a balance of power between them
(Xen. *Hell.* 2.3.41; Diod. Sic. 15.63).

109.5. dissension . . . rot . . . : i.e.'medism', which had been
feared since the first Persian landing in Greece . In particular,
Miltiades' political opponents, the Alcmaeonids, were suspected
of plotting to restore their power through Persian support. See
How & Wells II, 359–360. His arguments for joining battle are
thus purely political, and reflect his own political position. Callimachus, on the other hand, might be expected to have weighed the
military factors at least to some degree. These would include
assessment of the sizes of the two armies and the prospects of each
being augmented, the Persian by the arrival of the victorious
contingent from Eretria, the Athenian by the arrival of the

Spartans. Both sides had reasons to delay the engagement, but the Philaid tradition gives Miltiades personal credit for the decision to fight. It also (110) emphasises his constitutionalism, probably as a counterblast to accusations of tyrannical ambitions. His family's enmity with the Pisistratids (106) was regarded by some as rivalry.

Herodotus' narrative of the Battle of Marathon, though short of topographical detail and uninformative as to numbers and types of soldiers involved in the different phases of the fighting, generally gives a reasonably clear account, drawn from a contemporary tradition. That tradition favours the hoplite class, and sets the pattern for future generations of historians and orators, nearly all of whom accord higher praise to the heroes of Marathon than to the men of the lowest class who served in the ships at Salamis. But whether those heroes **advanced at a run towards the enemy, not less than a mile away** (112.1) must be doubted. This statement must be an exaggeration of a counter-tactic against the enemy's archers, some of whom would have been mounted. The hoplites were certainly trained in advancing at the .double, but in this case needed to do so only when within bowshot, at which distance the enemy might also begin to feel the first onset of terror at the spectacle. The forward movement would also help to mask the thinness of the Athenian centre.

114. Callimachus was killed, fighting bravely: Some famous names fell, like Homeric heroes (*Iliad* 13 and 14) fighting round the ships; but the Persians got away without too much difficulty. Were they already preparing to sail, and was it only a small advanced contingent of Athenians that reached them before they embarked? Embarkation may even have begun before the battle, and indeed have been the reason why the Athenians attacked when they did. After their initial success, there was no time to complete mopping-up operations; that was why they **left the defeated enemy to make their escape** (113.2) after their victory on the wings. The urgency of the Athenian departure for Athens is not immediately apparent, since the distance **round Sunium for Athens** (115), about 70 miles, could probably not have been covered in under 12 hours, leaving ample time for the Athenians to march from Marathon to Athens. But the whole of the Persian expeditionary force was not engaged at Marathon. Where was Artaphernes? If he was not still at Eretria, he may have been on his way to Athens; or at least Miltiades may have feared that he was.

117. The numbers are traditional and probably accurate. It has been suggested that the figures on the Parthenon frieze ('Elgin

Marbles') may represent the Athenian dead—mortals for the first time immortalised in temple sculpture. Their names were probably recorded on *stêlai* erected on the site of the battle, where they were buried. Most of the Persian dead were those who had attacked the Athenian centre and were engulfed.

120. two thousand Spartans set off for Athens: The Spartans were alerted by Philippides on the ninth day of the lunar month, marched on the 14th or 15th (the middle of the month when the moon was full), and arrived in Attica on the 17th or 18th, having marched some 150 miles in three days.

121. The tale of the Alcmaeonidae: The purpose of the shield-signal (115) was probably to encourage the Persians to attack Athens directly from the sea, presumably because the medising traitors there, supporters of Hippias, had matured their plans. The belief that the Alcmaeonids were prominent among the medisers arose not only from their unpopularity, but also from their association with tyrants and eastern trade sources. See W.G. Forrest, 'Herodotos and Athens', *Phoenix* 38 (1984) 3. H's heavy reliance upon Alcmaeonid sources makes him a biased commentator, and his reasoning in this chapter is not founded on historical fact: for example, the Alcmaeonid Cleisthenes had held office under Hippias (see Penguin Introd. p.32). But no solid evidence implicating the Alcmaeonids has been found.

125–131. This story of the origin of the wealth of the Alcmaeonids has a popular, comic flavour. Gold, greed, opportunism and ingenuity are better ingredients for a good tale than more prosaic reasons for Alcmaeonid wealth such as profitable trading with Lydia during the period of her greatest prosperity. Personalities too: the fabulously wealthy Croesus, Alcmaeon, (juxtaposed at some expense to chronology (see How & Wells II, p.116)), Cleisthenes, Hippocleides. The story of the suitors of Agariste also belongs to the age of aristocratic ideals in which men of wealth compete in a variety of physical and artistic activities in order to affirm their claims to power. See O. Murray, *Early Greece*, (Fontana, 1980) 202–203. A further attraction of the story is the behaviour of Hippocleides, which betrays a moral flaw of the kind which the lyric poet Pindar frequently warned his aristocratic patrons against. It is a *hybris-nemesis* story of aristocratic folly, and as such would have delighted H's popular audiences, while his aristocratic friend would have pointed out that Cleisthenes viewed the young suitor's behaviour with gravity.

132. Miltiades' disastrous expedition to Paros provided H with his favourite ending to a tale of a successful career. He asks for a fleet **without even telling the Athenians the object of the expedition**, conceals his real reason, which is personal (133), commits a sacrilegious act (134), and receives the wound that kills him. By focussing on the island on which Miltiades met with disaster, H may have ignored a decision by the Athenians to mount a comprehensive expedition against all the islands which had given earth and water to Datis (Cornelius Nepos, *Miltiades* 7 following Ephorus, Frg.107, F.H.G.i.263). The strategic reasons for this expedition, as for the later one by Themistocles, were probably to block future western maritime advances by the Persians and to discourage the islanders from providing them with harbourage. By adopting the Parian version of events on that island, of which his Alcmaeonid friends would also have approved, H is able to introduce his favourite themes of sacrilege and divine retribution; but his version also contains some essential details: the number of ships (**seventy**, 135), the duration of the expedition (**twenty-six days**,135), and perhaps most important, the identity of the chief political opponent (**especially Xanthippus**, 136), who prosecuted Miltiades on his return. Xanthippus was a leading member of the Alcmaeonid family by marriage and the father of Pericles, and had no doubt taken advantage of Miltiades' absence to undermine his position.

THE GREAT PERSIAN INVASIONS

Book 7: To Thermopylae
1.1. to make war on Greece: On the previous expedition, Darius had hoped to induce some Greek states to give tokens of submission, and to subdue those that refused (6.94), but probably had no firm plans beyond the conquest of Athens and Eretria (C. Hignett, *Xerxes' Invasion of Greece*, (Oxford, 1963) 87). Now the defeat of his army by Athenian hoplites, if unavenged, threatened the security of the western flank of his empire. Hence the scale of the new preparations, and the time they took — **three years** (1.2), i.e. to 488/7. The **rebellion in Egypt** took place in 487.
    4. thirty-six years: From 522/1 to 486. For his accession, see 3.85–88.
        5.1. Xerxes at first was not at all interested in invading Greece: By casting Xerxes in the role of the hesitant or reluctant invader, H provides a credible context for the long debate which follows. But as heir to Darius' unfinished business along with his throne, and having witnessed his elaborate preparations, Xerxes cannot

have put the invasion of Greece to the back of his mind for long. The **argument for revenge** needed stating for the benefit not of Xerxes, who uses it himself (8.a 2, b 2), but of H's readers. It was by far the strongest short-term motive for this invasion, and beside it the influence of the Pisistratids, the Aleuadae, and even that of Mardonius, the King's cousin, pale into insignificance; though the different points of view of these persuaders provides H with a varied collection of arguments. But even with all this material at his disposal, H never allows the central figure of the King to recede for long from the foreground. It is his character and motivation that are explored most thoroughly, and rightly so, since he is the fountain-head of all decisive thought and action.

8. Xerxes called a conference of the leading men in the country: The length and literary artistry of this debate should not be allowed to obscure the fact that H could not possibly have had any clear knowledge of it. Rather, these qualities indicate the importance he attached to the dramatic presentation of motives, causes, character and the power of persuasion. These chapters provided models for later historians, notably Livy. The duty to record 'what was said' no less faithfully than 'what was done', so clearly enunciated by Thucydides (1.22.1), was no less readily recognised and discharged by Herodotus. Speeches and conversations, as well as providing variety of literary genre, convey reasoning and argument more forcefully and naturally than narrative. See F.W. Walbank, *Speeches in Greek Historians*: 3rd J.L. Myres Memorial Lecture, Oxford, 1965.

8 a 1–2. never yet remained inactive . . . how not to fall short of the kings . . . before me: Thus H identifies the chief general or long-term cause of wars involving barbarian potentates. Like Croesus (1.73.1), Xerxes has a craving for the expansion of his empire. H is right to set this cause at the beginning of the debate, emphasising the barbarian obsession with material wealth here as in the Solon-Croesus dialogue (1.29–33). No less important for the interpretation of later events, the speech has the immediate function of characterising the *hybris* of Xerxes (**we shall so extend the empire of Persia**, 8 c 1), lays down the terms of the debate, and possibly influences the advice which he receives from his counsellors. In this connection, the position of Mardonius is of particular interest: is he merely flattering, compliant and uncritical like the majority of the King's advisers, or is H following a genuine tradition which made him the strongest advocate of the invasion? Perhaps H is exaggerating his influence at the beginning of Xerxes' reign in order to make the task of the tragic warner, Artabanus, seem more difficult and dangerous, and therefore more dramatically effective.

9 a 1. Have we anything to fear from them? The size of their army? Their wealth?: Laying characteristic barbarian emphasis on material resources, Mardonius has to fall back on the argument that the Greeks lack judgement and organisation in matters of war. As with many caricatures (which this is), an element of truth lies at its heart, and this is brought out as the narrative unfolds. It has even been suggested (How & Wells II, 129), that H was expressing his own view in the words **they ought to be able to find a better way of settling their differences** (9 b 2). But Mardonius' assessment of the prospects of success is wildly one-sided, omitting all mention of Marathon and the five-year duration of the Ionian revolt. His *hybris* is even more blatant than that of the King.

10.1. For a while nobody dared to put forward the opposite view: In the Greek democracies of the fifth century, especially Athens, freedom of speech found literary counterparts in sophistic writings which were attaining heights of popularity when H was writing his history. They were published as pairs of speeches arguing the same issue from opposing standpoints. It was left to Thucydides to adapt this method of presenting arguments in its purest form to historiography, but its possibilities were not lost on Herodotus. The Persian court was hardly an ideal environment in which to explore those possibilities, but his choice of **Artabanus taking courage from . . . his relationship . . . Xerxes' uncle** gives sufficient credibility to the dialogue, and supplies a literary ingredient which his Athenian audiences would recognise from drama—the unheeded prophet of doom personified in Teiresias and Cassandra.

10 a 3. But you, my lord, mean to attack a nation greatly superior to the Scythians: An example of 'comparative argument', listed in later rhetorical handbooks. The use of historical examples to illustrate an argument was also extensive in later Greek oratory.

10 d 2. lay his plans carefully . . . e 1. Gods . . . envy of their pride . . . f. Haste is the mother of failure . . . g. Slander is a wicked thing: Artabanus' concluding words are full of sentiments current in Athenian literature. Its prophetic ending has literary parallels in Homer and the tragic poets.

11.1. Xerxes was exceedingly angry: the characterisation of Xerxes now begins in earnest. The impetuous, quixotic side of his nature is to dominate his actions, but a reflective, diffident side is allowed to appear. When he says **My understanding has hardly yet grown to its full strength . . . hot young blood . . . young man**

(13.2), he has been on the throne for four years and is in his late thirties, so H may here be drawing on a Greek literary stereotype which associates such qualities as he wishes to ascribe to Xerxes with young men. This partly explains his behaviour to H's readers, makes him into a more credible character, and even excites some sympathy by representing him as vulnerable (**those who would force me into this war do not leave me alone for a moment**).

The dream-story adds a further, decisive element. The way H tells it leaves no doubt that he thought Artabanus' initial judgement on dreams, that **they do not come from God** (16 b 2), to have been discredited by events. It has even been suggested that Artabanus, while expressing a 'modern' view of dreams, has not completely freed himself of the older way of thinking about them as having a kind of independent existence, when he speaks of them as **drifting phantoms** (E.R. Dodds, *The Greeks and the Irrational*, (Berkeley, 1951) 118). With all doubt removed that the dreams conveyed an urgent divine command, and Artabanus in this case not so much unheeded as silenced in his attempt to **turn aside the course of destiny** (17.2), Xerxes is in a similar situation to Polycrates of Samos (3.40–44): he has passed the point of no return, and nothing he may do can avert disaster. It is as if the gods have taken over, as they often do in Homer. This idea of superior powers predetermining the course of events is central to H's view of history.

19.1. The Magi . . . portended the conquest of the world: These priests were under pressure not only from Xerxes, who **had made his decision to fight**, but also apparently from divine powers, who were equally determined that he should go. Yet the dream contained obviously discouraging signs—the vanishing crown of olive, suggesting both the outcome and the agent of doom, Athens. This final dream and its interpretation completes the divine plot: it is not a warning but a confirmation of the will of the gods.

20.1. For the four years following the conquest of Egypt . . . close of the fifth: Xerxes subdued Egypt in 485, assembled his host at Sardis in autumn 481, and set out for Greece the following spring, nearly five years after he began his preparations. For the chronology of his march to Thermopylae, see K.J. Sacks, 'Herodotus and the Dating of Thermopylae', *Classical Quarterly* 26 (1976) 232ff.

20.2. The army was indeed far greater . . . : Thucydides agrees, even while he is trying to magnify the importance of the Peloponnesian War. On Darius' Scythian Campaign, see 4.83–98; for

Scythian incursions into Media, see 1.103–106; 4.1–13.

20.2. the armies which the stories tell us Agamemnon and Menelaus led to Troy: Like Thucydides (1.10), H regarded the Trojan War as historical, and shared his scepticism concerning the numbers recorded in the Homeric Catalogue (*Iliad* 2.484ff.).

22.1. past three years . . . cutting a canal: The canal was begun in 483. It was some 2500 yards long, and cut mainly through sandy soil on low-lying ground. H affirms that it was both completed (37) and used (122). Its construction makes good sense if Xerxes was intending the permanent occupation of Greece; it also met the needs of his invasion strategy, the central principle of which was close cooperation between fleet and army. H's dismissal of the operation as **mere ostentation** (24) therefore seems rash. It betrays the desire he shares with other authors to show the *hybris* of Xerxes at every opportunity. Hauling the whole Persian fleet across the isthmus of Athos, as he suggests, would have been impractically time-consuming.

H gives a minimum of detail about one of the most intriguing aspects of the invasion—the problem of supplying so vast a host with food and water. Regarding the latter, it is likely that the rhetorical 'drank rivers dry' had its origin in real water shortage at various points in the march through Thrace. As to food, some of the supply dumps which he describes were probably sited at convenient marching distances from the local sources of food on which the Persians drew heavily.

27.1. Pythius, the son of Atys was thus the grandson of the Lydian king Croesus. His story is the familiar one of fabulous wealth leading to ruin, but with some important additions. His particular brand of arrogance causes him to ask a preposterous favour of the King, forgetting that he is his mere subject and slave (38–40). The story also serves, more importantly, to add to the characterisation of Xerxes by portraying his interest in Pythius' material wealth, his generosity, his absolutism and his cruelty. H exploits to the full the story's dramatic elements, particularly Xerxes' sudden change from friendliness to anger, and Pythius' prospects of even greater wealth and royal favour abruptly shattered by the killing of his eldest son.

35.2. barbarous and presumptuous words: The whipping of the Hellespont was regarded by the Greeks as Xerxes' worst act of sacrilege after the destruction of their temples. Although the infliction of punishment on inanimate objects or irrational creatures was not a peculiarly Persian custom, this particular victim was, like other 'rivers', to Greek minds a god; and Xerxes was treating it like a runaway slave (**fetters . . . lashes**). The act of bridging it was seen as a form of bondage (Aeschylus, *Persians* 745-7).

36.1. galleys and triremes . . . moored slantwise to the Black Sea: i.e. with their prows facing the current, which flows outwards from the Black Sea and was thereby afforded the smoothest possible passage. By building the bridges at an oblique angle to the current, the engineers reduced their resistance to it still further. **The cables** (36.3) served both to bind the ships together and to provide continuous 'rails' to which the planks were fixed. Being at two different crossing-points, the bridges were not equal in length. H unfortunately provides no information as to precisely how the bridges were assembled, an operation requiring exceptional skill, teamwork and coordination. Otherwise, however, his description is careful enough to enable the reader to form a mental picture.

37.2. the sun vanished: This eclipse probably belongs to the year 481 rather then 480. If this was so, it would have been seen when Xerxes left Sousa. Xerxes will have found the interpretation of the Magi especially convincing if he knew (as he may well have done) that the moon actually caused the eclipse of the sun.

39.3. Pythius' eldest son was killed for perhaps two reasons: to punish Pythius for his presumption and to provide a prize sacrificial victim at the start of the expedition.

41.2. Persian infantry ten thousand strong: These were the Immortals, so called because casualties among them were immediately replaced (83).

43.1. the Scamander, familiar to H's readers from Homer, became a narrow stream well before high summer, as did most other rivers along the route to Greece. See p.454 n. Troy (Ilion) was a Greek settlement at this time (Troy VIII). **Trojan Athene**, the city's (vain) protectress in Homer (*Iliad* 6.269, 297ff.), was still worshipped there in the time of Xenophon (*Hell.* 1.1.4) and Alexander the Great (Arrian, *Anab.* 1.11.7). Who were the **great men of old** (43.2)? Perhaps the Trojan heroes, whom the Persians may have identified as 'Asiatics'(1.4.2-4) like themselves, and ancient enemies of the Greeks.

45. congratulated himself—and the moment after burst into tears: H takes every opportunity to add to his portrait of Xerxes. His purpose is to furnish him with sympathetic qualities to balance the mercurial, tempestuous character of a man intoxicated with power and so make him more like one of the heroes of Greek tragic drama, who typically are men of complex character. Indeed, the conversation with Artabanus has a strong flavour of tragedy,

with the older man cast in the role of the tragic chorus (How &
Wells II,148), voicing pessimistic views about life and the human
condition. Such views also occur frequently in earlier Greek
literature, reflecting in particular the hard conditions of rural life,
and sounding strange coming from a privileged Persian of the royal
house. Xerxes' own more positive and optimistic approach may
reflect a contemporary Persian view of life based on their religious
beliefs.

49.1. enemies . . . the land and the sea: The problems of
mounting major operations in a distant foreign land are given a
prophetic flavour and linked to the contrasting ideas of fore-
thought and trusting to luck. The essential difficulties are well
summarised. The fleet needed to hug the coast, both in order to
maintain contact with the army and to replenish supplies, especially of fresh water. Coastal storms took a heavy toll of those
ships that were unable to find safe harbourage. On land, 'living off
the land' was difficult in sparsely populated country, as must have
been the supply of food to the dumps on the route (25); while in
more thickly populated regions, the common danger tended to
unite the inhabitants (Thuc. 6.33.5), so that the enemy's numbers
grew with each mile of the advance, while those of the invader
were diminished by hunger (Aeschylus, *Persians* 792–4).

**51.2. on no account to take these Ionians to attack men of their
own blood**: The possible danger of mass treachery did not mate-
rialise, even in the heat of battle (8.85), in spite of the urgent
entreaties of Themistocles (8.22). Only when total defeat was
imminent did the Ionians desert the Persians (9.103).

55.2. The first to cross were the Ten Thousand: The opposite
order from that of the army when leaving Sardis. Two motives for
the described order, which H presumably preferred to the version
in which **the king crossed last** (55.3), seem possible: firstly, that
Xerxes and his best troops should have the honour of landing first
on European soil; and secondly, that the crossing be speeded by
the presence of Xerxes on the far side. The whips also served that
purpose, and further remind the reader that this was an army of
slaves. The ironic juxtaposition of contrasting events—the likening
of Xerxes to Zeus and the omens to whose significance he was
blinded by his *atê* (infatuation) add a colourful literary touch. In
Greece, the **hare** was associated with living a hunted existence
(3.108.3; Demosthenes, *On the Crown* 263).

58.1. The fleet . . . orders to wait: Following the central strategy
of close military and naval cooperation.

60.1. The total of **1,700,000** for the army is generally regarded as impossibly high (see C. Hignett, *Xerxes' Invasion of Greece,* (Oxford, 1963) 350–355; henceforth Hignett). It would nevertheless have been possible for that number to cross easily in seven days and nights (56.1). Marching at 3 m.p.h., spaced at one yard, one column of 1400 men would cross the 1400 yd. distance in 15.9 minutes. In 7 days (168 hours, 10080 minutes), the number crossing, in a single column over the upper bridge (55.1), would be 887,547. That figure would, of course be multiplied by the number of columns sent across the bridge, which was not much less than a ship's length wide. Rejection of the high ancient estimates of the size of Xerxes' forces stems mainly from considerations of supply and organisation rather than from a belief that such vast sources of manpower were not available to him. H's catalogue of the army in chs. 61–88 has a Homeric parallel (*Iliad* 2.494–877), and perhaps serves literary as much as historical purposes. Its motley cosmopolitanism, with six broad ethnic divisions and as many as eighteen types of armour, suggests military impracticality, but he emphasises that **the native Persians were not only the best but also the most magnificently equipped** (83.2). In the battles that follow it is these who perform the most signal deeds of valour on the barbarian side. The different races of the barbarian world, their customs and appearance are an abiding interest in the *History*, and H researched this catalogue with great thoroughness; but most of these colourful contingents are not heard of again.

89–99. The following list corresponds with the total of 1207. That number is derived from Aeschylus, *Persians*, 341ff., but the poet is referring to the Persian fleet at Salamis. The Persians suffered heavy losses in storms (7.188–190 (400 ships); 8.12–13 (the 200 ships which sailed south to round Euboea, plus those damaged at anchor in Aphetae)). H states it as his opinion (8.66) that reinforcements made up these losses before the great sea battle, but the vague terms in which he makes this claim do not inspire confidence, and the Greek states he lists could certainly not have mustered 600 ships. He is trying to reconcile two traditions: that of the great size of the barbarian fleet, in order to magnify the achievement of the Greeks; and that of the storms, in order to suggest that the gods were on the side of the Greeks and angry with Xerxes for his sacrilegious treatment of the Hellespont. Both the total before losses (1207) and the losses themselves are likely to be exaggerations. Hignett (p.350) suggests 600 as the number of Persian ships at the beginning of the invasion, of which about 200 were destroyed in the storms.

99. Artemisia . . . the daughter of Lygdamis, a Halicarnassian: Hence a fellow-citizen of Herodotus, who ruled during his early years; but more importantly, an historical personality to be conjured with for literary purposes: another adviser for Xerxes, but also a woman with masculine characteristics, recalling some of the most memorable heroines of Greek tragedy—Clytemnestra in Aeschylus, *Agamemnon* and Antigone in Sophocles, *Antigone*.

100-104. Having completed his description of Xerxes' vast armament, H turns to dialogue, further enhancing the variety thus achieved by making Demaratus dwell upon moral rather than material concepts, and upon the Greek standpoint after so much description devoted to the barbarians. His generalisation **poverty is my country's inheritance from of old, but valour she won for herself by wisdom and the strength of law. By her valour Greece now keeps both poverty and bondage at bay** (102.1) is a description of Greece after the fall of the tyrants, which Sparta did much to encourage. His subsequent remarks refer mainly to his fellow-Spartans, and they prepare us for the supreme expression of Spartan valour at Thermopylae, where their hoplites vindicate his claim that **fighting together they are the best soldiers in the world** (104.4). The essence of hoplite fighting was concerted action, mutual protection and instant but voluntary obedience to commands. Xerxes contributes little of substance to this dialogue: he has already shown incomprehension that men should regard the defence of their freedom as necessary, and death preferable to the loss of it.

105-107. Examples of barbarians no less brave than Greeks, but motivated by fear (107.1. **afraid the king might think . . .**). But Boges (cf. Thuc. 1.98) wins the admiration of H, who also notes with approval how the Persian kings rewarded their loyal captains. But the manner of Boges' death is typical of a barbarian potentate.

The westward advance of Xerxes' army was relatively uneventful because earlier Persian expeditions had subdued most of the natives, two exceptions being the Satrae (111.1) and the king of the Bisaltae (8.116). The army marched in three divisions (121), i.e. three parallel columns, to reduce the inordinate length (A.R. Burn, *Persia and the Greeks*, (London, 1962) 337). The elaborate and expensive preparations demanded by Xerxes for his entertainment (118-20) portray his vain arrogance, but also reflect the wealth of the region, especially in gold and silver, which was exploited by the islanders of Thasos, who established settlements for the purpose at Stryme and elsewhere. (On the wealth of Thasian mines, both those on the island and those on the mainland, see 6.46).

121. Acanthus was a vitally important staging-post, since it had one of the very few protected harbours on this coast. Up to this point close contact had been maintained between fleet and army, and **the fleet passed through the Athos canal**(122) in accordance with this strategy. But thence it sailed south, west and north-west while the army marched across Chalcidice. They reunited at Therma (modern Thessaloniki, 123–4) probably in early August. The presence of **lions** (125) in this part of Greece is attested by Aristotle (*Hist. Anim.* 6.31,519a) and Pliny, *Nat. Hist.* 8.45, but Dio Chrysostom Orat. 21,269c says that they had disappeared from Europe by his time (c.A.D.120).

129.4. and the story is a reasonable one; for if one believes . . . :H shows his usual respect for popular tradition, but may seem to conceal his personal view of its religious side with the condition "if one believes. . . ." It could be argued, however, that in saying that the story as a whole, which incorporates belief in Poseidon as the god of earthquakes, is 'reasonable', he is implying that belief in Poseidon as the god of earthquakes is reasonable. Probably a distinction must be drawn between his views on natural phenomena for which he believes scientific explanation may be found, and which he enjoys explaining (e.g. 2.25–27), and those of a more sudden and catastrophic nature like earthquakes and the thunderbolts and rock-falls at Delphi (8.38), especially when the latter could be attributed to divine wrath at some human action.

130.2. The Thessalians . . . made their submission to me in good time . . . : Their decision was in fact made only after they had ascertained that the other Greeks would not rally to their defence (172–4, where H is careful to show that the medising Aleuadae, though they had convinced Xerxes otherwise, did not represent the views of most leading Thessalians. See How & Wells I,40; Hignett, 102–103). In giving the full list of medising states (132.1) H ignores the time factor: the Thebans and Locrians did not medise until after Thermopylae.

132.2. the Greeks who determined to resist the invader swore an oath: At their Congress, held at the Isthmus of Corinth (Diod. Sic. 11.3), in one of a number of meetings there since the leaders of the patriotic states first met at Sparta in Autumn 481. See 145.1.

133.2. I do not myself believe that this happened as a direct result of their crime: i.e. the wholesale destruction was an excessive punishment for this offence, and a graver reason must be found. H supplies it in 5.102: the burning of the temple of Cybebe at Sardis. Much more striking is the story of the delayed vengeance of Talthybius (137), for in the course of it H makes one of his clearest

statements about the gods: **and in this, I think, the hand of god was
clearly to be seen . . . this, to me at least, is clear evidence of divine
intervention**.

With this inspiring story of Spartan patriotism, containing the
perennial contrast between Greek love of freedom and the barbarian acceptance of slavery, symbolised by the custom of prostra-
tion (136), and his overt statement of opinion (139) about
Athenian resolution and its importance for Greek success, H sets
the stage for the main conflict by anticipating the contributions of
the two states to which, in his view, the Greeks owed the most.
And he restates the view (138.1, cf. 54. 2) that Xerxes intended **the
conquest of the whole of Greece**. The strategic and political
assessment of the situation in 481–480 B.C. (138–139) prior to
the conflict is broadly in agreement with that expressed by
Thucydides through the mouths of Athenian envoys to Sparta and
opposed by Corinthian envoys (Thuc. 1.68–78). A combined land
and sea force must inevitably overcome a defending army un-
protected by a navy, especially when it enjoys numerical superiority. The Athenian fleet was the most important single factor in
frustrating the Persian westerly advance; and it was Greek naval
supremacy after Salamis that compelled Mardonius to force an
early decision on land in unfavourable circumstances.

139.6. the terrifying warnings of the oracle at Delphi: Neither
prophesy offered much encouragement to the Athenians, even on
the most optimistic interpretation. The extreme pessimism of the
first oracle reflects the rational belief of the Delphic authorities in
certain Persian victory and the destruction of Athens. Mention of
Salamis in the second (141.4) raises the difficult question of
chronology, for no prediction could have been made of a sea-
battle so far south when the Greek fleet was preparing to face the
enemy in northern waters. It is also bafflingly ambiguous, but this
is perhaps an argument for its authenticity, and H's account of the
discussion provoked by the phrase 'wooden walls' has a historical
ring about it. Furthermore, by introducing Themistocles into the
argument, he supplies us with a possible influence behind the
oracle; but it is unwise, on the available evidence, to assume that
he did more than interpret it to suit his strategic aims. We later
learn that he had a contingency plan for the use of the ships if his
naval strategy was rejected by the other Greeks: to use them to
transport his fellow-citizens westwards to start a new life (8.62.2)
as the Phocaeans had done. It may have been with this precedent
in mind that the first oracle advised the Athenians to **Fly to
the world's end** (140).

143.1. Themistocles called Neocles' son: Though lacking connections with the dynastic families of Athens, his family was not undistinguished in his own deme of Phrearrhioi, and he was probably archon in 493/2. The downfall and death of Miltiades left him with less formidable opponents, against whom he successfully used the device of ostracism. See R.J. Lenardon, *The Saga of Themistocles* (London, 1978), 49. By 483 he was the most influential Athenian politician, and was able to press forward with his naval policy. This involved the building of a new harbour at Piraeus, but this work was not completed until after the war (Thuc. 1.93.2). Thucydides names foresight, judgement and ability to explain his plans as his special qualities (1.138.3). Certainly his oratorical powers must have been impressive, and his greatest persuasive achievement was to have convinced the Spartans that the Greeks should direct their greatest efforts towards a naval victory. To this should be added his persuading the Athenians to enlarge the navy instead of distributing the money from Laurium among themselves (p. 490); and finally, by winning acceptance for his interpretation of the 'wooden wall', he was able to enact a decree for the evacuation of Athens and the manning of the navy, perhaps as early as September 481. (So N.G.L. Hammond, 'The Narrative of Herodotus VII and the Decree of Themistocles at Troezen', *Journal of Hellenic Studies* 102 (1982) 82–93). The text of a decree of Themistocles was discovered in 1959 on a 3rd-century inscription at Troezen, and the question of its authenticity has been discussed voluminously ever since. For a review of this literature, see A.J. Podlecki, *The Life of Themistocles* (Montreal & London, 1975) 147–167. H's attitude to Themistocles is two-sided: he accords him full credit when events render it unavoidable, but in general tends to follow sources hostile to him, beginning with the present one which seems to hint at illegitimacy.

144.1. the mines at Laurium: In southern Attica, close by Themistocles' own deme of Phrearrheoi. They had been worked since at least Mycenaean times (Bronze Age). See J.F. Healy, *Mining and Metallurgy in the Greek and Roman World* (London, 1978) 78ff.

145.1. The conference of Greek states: The initiative for this conference came officially from Sparta, but Athenian counsels, probably led by Themistocles, played a significant part (139.5). The conference took place in autumn 481 if it coincided with the arrival of Xerxes in Sardis (145.2). The venue was probably the Isthmus of Corinth. On the constitution and other questions from other sources. The Greek position was even more vulnerable than H describes: in addition to the pass near Gonnus, there were two more distant but more easily negotiable passes to the west, at Petra and BVolustana, which Xerxes probably used in his advance. Defence of more than one pass would have required more Greek infantry, and proportionally more Thessalian commitment to the Greek cause. Sparta's doubts about this and her own reluctance to defend a distant outpost are reflected in their appointment of **Euanetus son of Carenus . . . not of the royal blood** to lead their contingent. It may well be that H did not realise, or did not wish to admit, the full extent of Persian influence in Thessaly at this time. See Hignett, 102–103; Burn, 341–343.; and esp. N. Robertson, 'The Thessalian Expedition of 480 B.C.', *Journal of Hellenic Studies* 96 (1976) 100–120.

175.2. communication would be easy: Cooperation between fleet and army was as essential to Greek strategy as it was to Persian.

176.3. to the south-west—inland . . . other side of the roadway: H actually writes **to the west . . . to the east**, apparently not realising that the direction of the road is east and west. But his topography of both Thermopylae and Artemisium is otherwise admirably clear, when allowance is made for later geological changes.

177. Pieria: The country through which one approaches the passes into Thessaly, north of Mount Olympus. The Greeks left themselves with little time to spare.

178.1. Pray to the winds: Another piece of Delphic ambiguity, made to serve a literary purpose by Herodotus, who, like a tragic poet, foreshadows major events with minor ones and lays signposts for his audience. They may now hear of the defeat at Thermopylae in the knowledge that a reversal of fortune is to follow with the wrecking of part of the Persian fleet in a storm.

179. ten of the fastest ships were sent ahead both to look out for the Greeks and to check that the waters were safe (cf. 183.2). This first encounter may have begun after the Persians surprised the Greeks at dawn in the harbour after a night approach (so Hignett, 160, following Munro in *Cambridge Ancient History* iv.285). But if it took place in open water, the Persian success showed that their ships were swifter and more effective than the Greek triremes in such conditions, and must have influenced subsequent Greek strategy.

181.1. Pytheas of Aegina reappears at Salamis (8.92). Leon of Troezen was apparently sacrificed as the first-fruit of victory, but H's reference to his name (= Lion) implies that he thought animal

relating to the new confederacy, see P.A. Brunt, 'The Hellenic League against Persia', *Historia* 2 (1953) 135–163.

146–147. The story of Xerxes' treatment of the Greek spies does not so much reveal the nobler side of his character (so How & Wells II,187), as continue the theme of his *hybris*, but with the refinement of psychological acumen. There is no mention of clemency towards the spies: they are designated as instruments of propaganda. H confirms the continuity in his portrayal of Xerxes by referring back to his expression of **a similar opinion on another occasion** (147.2).

148.2. The Argives themselves explain . . . : And H does not comment adversely on their explanation. Their fear and enmity was solely against Sparta, since their bloody defeat at the Battle of Sepeia (c.495 B.C.: 6.76ff.). Their refusal to serve under the command of their recent bitter adversary is understandable. Later Argos was a potential or actual ally of Athens, being like her a democracy. H suspends condemnation of her medism for as long as he can, but is later forced to admit it in the face of more damning evidence (8.73.3).

148.4. By right Argos was entitled to the sole command : This right was claimed by virtue of the legend that the founding hero of Argos, Temenos, was the eldest of the three sons of the Heraclid Aristomachus who cast lots for the lands of the Peloponnese.

151. Callias . . . on quite different business: Negotiations with Persia perhaps intended to lead to the signing of a formal treaty ending hostilities, the so-called Peace of Callias (449/8). See Russell Meiggs, *The Athenian Empire* (Oxford, 1973) 129–151, 487–495, 598–599; E. Badian, 'The Peace of Callias', *Journal of Hellenic Studies* 107 (1987) 1–39.

152.3. My business is to record what people say, but I am by no means bound to believe it: Here implying disbelief, but enunciating the central principle governing the inclusion of material, and confirming previous statements (2.123.2; 4.195.2) denying editorial responsiblity.

153.2. the Earth Goddesses: Demeter and her daughter Persephone. These deities were especially honoured in a land where corn was the chief product, and the priests who presided over their rites enjoyed political as well as religious power.

154.1. Cleander seized power at Gela around 504. **Hippocrates** succeeded him in 498 and ruled until his death in 491, when he was succeeded by Gelon. But the latter did not become **master of Syracuse** until 485. By unifying much of eastern Sicily and central-ising it on Syracuse, Gelon created the only power in Sicily capable of successfully resisting Carthaginian expansion, which he did at the Battle of Himera in 480 (166).

157–161. Much of the substance of these speeches is the product of H's literary imagination: the hyperbolic **with all the armies of the east** (157.1); the maxim that **well-laid plans have a prosperous issue** (157.3); the Homeric references and the Athenian claim to be **the only nation never to have left the soil from which it sprang** (161.3), are hardly relevant to the negotiations in hand but calculated to be popular with H's Athenian audiences. Finally, Gelon himself is made to use imagery, **the spring of the year . . . is lost** (162.2), which was ascribed by later sources to Pericles (Aristotle, *Rhetoric* 1.7.34,3.10; Plut. *Pericles*, 8.28.) Pericles, like Churchill, may have borrowed extensively from earlier sources, but the link here is probably between him and H rather than between Gelon and an unknown earlier lyric poet. As to the actual negotiations, there is no reason to doubt that Gelon made extreme demands for the leadership, which were to some extent vindicated by his success against the Carthaginians. It may well be that, like the Argives, but for reasons of future security rather than past disasters, he was unwilling to put his armed forces at risk against an external enemy.

165.1. Terillus . . . brought into Sicily . . . an army 300,000 strong from Carthage . . . : The number seems suspiciously inflated in order to match Persian numbers opposing the Greeks on land. The tradition seems firm, however, that the Carthaginian force, consisting as usual of mercenaries, was large and well-equipped. This in turn raises the question of whether its landing, while technically a response to Terillus' invitation, was in fact the wholehearted seizure of an opportunity for which the Carthaginian leaders had been waiting to exploit a split among the Sicilian tyrants. Later Carthaginian history confirms their abiding interest in the island, with its rich resources of grain.

166.1. The Sicilians also maintain . . . on the same day: The fact that H is following the Sicilian view of these events should be remembered when considering whether the coincidence was purely accidental or not. There is a tradition preserved by Ephorus (fr.111) and Diodorus Siculus (11.1, derived from Timaeus) of some form of cooperation, perhaps even a formal alliance, between Xerxes and the Carthaginians. Scholarly opinion is fairly evenly divided: Burn (306) follows How & Wells (II,201) in accepting it, but Hignett regards the silence of Herodotus as decisive (95–96), while Hammond (*A History of Greece* (Oxford,

1959) 269) writes: 'it is unlikely that Persia feared any reinforce ment of Greece from Sicily, or that Carthage wished to see Persi conquer Greece and perhaps advance upon Sicily. Two furthe probability-arguments seem to support the latter view. H's Siciliar sources would surely have sought to magnify their achievement Himera by adding the danger of Persian complicity, if there ha been any; and the Persian armament was thought by Xerxes ar his chief advisers to be more than adequate for its task witho help from Carthage.

168.4. the prevailing north-easters or Etesian ('annual') win blew in August-September for about forty days, and the Battle Salamis was fought in late September. The Corcyreans w caught between two theatres of war, in Sicily and Greece, so th hesitation is hardly surprising. H's hostility towards them is pat (cf. 3.49–53), but Thucydides does not make the Corinthi reproach them with cowardice or treachery at this time in famous debate between them (1.37–43).

170.1. The story goes that Minos . . . : The historical counter to the legendary anger of Minos against Menelaus' people (i.e. Spartans or Peloponnesians) concerns the Cretan attempt colonisation, which met opposition from Spartan settler Tarentum (founded 707/6), as H describes. Minos addresse people as a god, as the Trojan War was **in the third gener after his death** (171.1). H is following Homeric chronology 13.451ff.; *Odyssey* 19.178ff.)

172.1. The Thessalians did not submit to Persia until they compelled: As Thessaly had no centralised government, unlikely that there was any unified direction of Thessalian p In deciding on their response, the Greeks must have cons **the intrigues of the Aleuadae** (7.6.2, 130.3), and wheth **Thessalian delegates** could guarantee their countrymen's s for the cause of Greek freedom, and indeed whether tha meant anything to the Thessalians in comparison with the self-preservation. Their decision to send north **10,000 infantry** (173.2), a substantial force, was based on three pri that it is better to fight as far as possible from one's ho (Plutarch, *Themistocles* 7); that it was better to face the b before he was joined by medising Greeks (including the Th and that mountain passes afford inferior numbers a bette of success than open terrain.

173.4. another way into Thessaly: H is surely right to p reason, for by now the Greeks must have had some idea o numbers, if not from the spies released by Xerxes (148

rather than human association with bravery and ferocity were in his captors' minds. But human sacrifice was common among the Persians, Phoenicians and other barbarian races, so it is likely that the choice of Leon as victim was due to an unfortunate etymological association.

183.1. fire-signal: See also 9.3. The most famous literary appearance of beacons is, of course, in Aeschylus, *Agamemnon* 280ff. For details of their use in ancient times, see Polybius 10.43ff.

184.1. I find by calculation: This suggests that the numbers are not based on Persian records. H accepts the traditional Aeschylean number of 1207 for the Persian fleet, and the numbers of naval personnel stem from that, on the assumption that each ship had a full complement. The total for both ships and their complements is probably too high, but not as preposterously so as those for the land forces (see 7.61ff. notes). Most of the numbers are, on H's own admission, mere estimates.

187.2. 110,340 bushels should read 110067½₂. See H & W II,213–214. Xerxes is plainly represented as a tragic figure at the height of his power immediately before the first of his disasters.

188.1. in lines, eight deep: With prows facing out to sea, to make maximum use of the mooring-space available, as explained by Homer, *Iliad* 14.33–37, where the Achaean ships are similarly drawn up. If the storm created on-shore waves, this was the best direction for them to be facing, but much of the damage would have been caused by the ships falling foul of one another.

189.1. Boreas: A god whose power was of increasing concern to the Athenians from the early fifth century, when growing maritime trade took their ships north-eastwards to the Black Sea. Note H's scepticism here: there had been an earlier storm which was not explained thus, but he feels obliged to record Athenian opinion.

190.1. Four hundred ships: i.e. naval ships, excluding merchantmen (cf. 191; so at 236.2, where Achaemenes mentions only the fighting ships). The tradition that both the Delphians and the Athenians prayed to the wind-gods probably embodies a later belief that the storms inflicted very great damage on the Persian fleet. Herodotus, believing the original number to have been 1207, may have heard that the gods destroyed one in three of the barbarian ships, and so arrived at his estimate.

murder of his son seems to suggest that Ameinocles himself was the killer, but the killing was probably accidental. As a vignette illustrating the swift succession of triumph and disaster, the story probably reminded H and his readers of Croesus' tragic loss of his son after boasting of his wealth to Solon (1.29–45).

196. the horses of Thessaly were renowned throughout Greece. But the superiority of Persian cavalry to the best Greece could offer (the only other Greeks with cavalry comparable to the Thessalian were the Boeotians, who also medised) materially affected subsequent Greek strategy.

197.1. Laphystian Zeus: or Zeus the Devourer. The legend and the ritual described is one of the few survivals of human sacrifice in Greece, where in historical times it was regarded with religious aversion.

198.1. tide: Although the Aegean is for the most part tideless, quite strong ebb-and-flow currents occur in certain narrow channels and gulfs in the north (cf. 8.129).

Herodotus' rather sketchy account of Xerxes' march from Therma to Thermopylae (198–200) is to be explained by the fact that it was largely unopposed, and perhaps also by H's limited knowledge of the topography of the area; though he did visit it.

202. The discrepancy between the 3100 Peloponnesians listed here and the 4000 in the epitaph (228) written soon after the battle and not likely to be an exaggeration, must be due to omissions by H, perhaps of *perioeci* or of men from Elis. Their numbers were still very small for the task they faced.

203. The Locrians of Opus . . . all they had: Estimated at 1000 by Ephorus, making the non-Peloponnesian contingent also 3100. The Theban contribution of 400 is notably small.

204. Leonidas traced his descent: Genealogies like this were reserved for men of heroic distinction, in the Homeric tradition (e.g. *Iliad* 10.68). See 8.131,139; 9.64.

205.2. fathers of living sons: Explained sufficiently by national policy of preserving the families of pure Spartan stock (*Spartiatai*), whose male members formed the backbone of their army. The defence of the pass at Thermopylae was probably seen as a compromise by the Spartans, as by the other Greeks; but it was a compromise fraught with imponderables. The Greeks to east and north of the Peloponnese insisted on all-Greek defence of their land, but how many of them would remain steadfast? Nevertheless, the pass afforded a good chance that their loyalty would never need to be tested. Events proved that it could have been defended with a very small force, since treachery was needed finally to turn the Greek position. Hence the Spartan contingent of only three hundred, matched by similar numbers from other states, was sufficient to stop the Persian advance through the narrow passage, and the stand was made as part of a concerted plan to keep Xerxes out of Greece (176.2) without thought of failure or self-sacrifice. H perhaps did not make up his mind about Thermopylae. He and later historians (Diod. Sic. 11.4.3–4, following Ephorus) were influenced by the oracle which demanded the death of a Heraclid king as the price for the preservation of Sparta (220). Although this would have been satisfied by the death of Leonidas alone, it introduced fatalistic elements into the story, which were as attractive to historians as to contemporaries who sought excuses for the defeat. For the different views on the aims and motives surrounding the campaign, see Hignett 113ff., esp. 124–5.

207. It was proposed . . . : The Peloponnesian proposal to fall back on the Isthmus is rejected by Macan and Hignett as unhistorical. In noting Peloponnesian isolationism, however, H directs no criticism at Sparta.

208.3. combing their hair: One of many curious stories intended by H to underline the fundamental difference in outlook of Greeks and barbarians. The martial preparations of the Spartans, who wore their hair long, stem from a self-imposed discipline and willing patriotism. They also have a ritual quality: a battle is treated like a form of festival celebration (cf. Xenophon, *Spartan Institutions* 11.3; 13.8). The warriors' contemptuous disregard for the spy reminds us of Demaratus' prediction (102.3) that the Spartans would fight, whatever the size of the army opposed to them.

210.1. For four days Xerxes waited: The fact may be accepted, but hardly H's explanation, which merely follows on from the King's conversation with Demaratus. The Greek position was in fact formidable, and neither Xerxes nor his army had experience in the specialised techniques of attacking a well-defended superior position. The eventual attack, far from being ordered by Xerxes in rage, may have been intended to test Greek strength. In the meantime he may also have been awaiting a favourable outcome at sea, and when this was not forthcoming, decided that the Greek army must be overcome at whatever cost.

211. The Spartan superiority over the barbarians in both training and equipment is briefly but vividly described in this chapter. The feigned retreat followed by a counter-charge was intended to bring the enemy to close quarters, where the superior armament of the hoplites took its toll, especially if the front was narrow and enemy numbers could not be used to advantage. See 9.62 for further discussion of Greek and Persian weaponry.

213.1. How to deal with the situation Xerxes had no idea: It would have been surprising if he had not consulted his generals,

but H represents him as acting alone, with no battle plan because
he had thought there would be no battle; viewing the proceedings
from afar, as at Salamis, and improvising tremulously as each new
situation arose.

Ephialtes or Epialtes. Once the tradition was established that
the army was betrayed by a Greek traitor, there were certain to be
counter-accusations, but other authorities agree with H, who
records the traitor's fate, complete with its twist of paradox, with
satisfaction.

215–219. The track . . . : H's description of the Persian ascent is
beautifully effective in its graphic simplicity, relying on paratactic
sentence structure and precise use of tenses. He breaks off his
narrative of the Persian march when they still have a long way to
go (end of 219 . . . **with all possible speed**). H is following mainly a
source sympathetic to Sparta, but Delphic influence is also present
as he is somewhat dismissive of the Phocians (cf.8.29; 9.17–18).
See Forrest, *art.cit.* (n. on 6.121) 7.

219.2. The army split . . . : Judgement as to which of the stories
was true depends on one's estimate of the strength of Leonidas'
authority. In 204, H says he is **in command of the whole army**
while **The contingents of the various states were under their own
officers**.

220.1. It is said . . . : The whole of this chapter is derived from
Spartan sources anxious to affirm the authority of Leonidas, the
resolution which Demaratus' account of the Spartan character
would lead readers to expect, and the divinely-ordained inevitability of defeat. These stories found general acceptance, and
Leonidas' stand was later praised even by Sparta's critics (e.g.
Isocrates, *Panegyricus* 92). H is careful, in his usual manner, to
mention the allegation that the Spartans were deserted by the
other Greeks, and his earlier narrative, by referring to a **council of
war** in which **opinions were divided** (219.2), seems to imply that
Leonidas, in the last resort, did not have the power to compel his
allies to stay and fight. Certainly they could not have detained the
Thebans **as hostages very much against their will** (222), and Plutarch's indignation at this slander of his fellow-countrymen (*On the
Malice of Herodotus* 31) is fully justified. But the Spartan tradition
did not entail criticism of any other Greeks, and it suited her allies
to accept her version of events. The oracle was probably a later
fabrication devised to justify the smallness of the Spartan force.

224.1. as those of men who deserve to be remembered: These
words recall the beginning of the *History*. The short narrative of the
final encounter is rich in Herodotean themes: religious observance;

relating to the new confederacy, see P.A. Brunt, 'The Hellenic League against Persia', *Historia* 2 (1953) 135–163.

146–147. The story of Xerxes' treatment of the Greek spies does not so much reveal the nobler side of his character (so How & Wells II,187), as continue the theme of his *hybris*, but with the refinement of psychological acumen. There is no mention of clemency towards the spies: they are designated as instruments of propaganda. H confirms the continuity in his portrayal of Xerxes by referring back to his expression of **a similar opinion on another occasion** (147.2).

148.2. The Argives themselves explain . . . : And H does not comment adversely on their explanation. Their fear and enmity was solely against Sparta, since their bloody defeat at the Battle of Sepeia (c.495 B.C.: 6.76ff.). Their refusal to serve under the command of their recent bitter adversary is understandable. Later Argos was a potential or actual ally of Athens, being like her a democracy. H suspends condemnation of her medism for as long as he can, but is later forced to admit it in the face of more damning evidence (8.73.3).

148.4. By right Argos was entitled to the sole command : This right was claimed by virtue of the legend that the founding hero of Argos, Temenos, was the eldest of the three sons of the Heraclid Aristomachus who cast lots for the lands of the Peloponnese.

151. Callias . . . on quite different business: Negotiations with Persia perhaps intended to lead to the signing of a formal treaty ending hostilities, the so-called Peace of Callias (449/8). See Russell Meiggs, *The Athenian Empire* (Oxford, 1973) 129–151, 487–495, 598–599; E. Badian, 'The Peace of Callias', *Journal of Hellenic Studies* 107 (1987) 1–39.

152.3. My business is to record what people say, but I am by no means bound to believe it: Here implying disbelief, but enunciating the central principle governing the inclusion of material, and confirming previous statements (2.123.2; 4.195.2) denying editorial responsiblity.

153.2. the Earth Goddesses: Demeter and her daughter Persephone. These deities were especially honoured in a land where corn was the chief product, and the priests who presided over their rites enjoyed political as well as religious power.

154.1. Cleander seized power at Gela around 504. **Hippocrates** succeeded him in 498 and ruled until his death in 491, when he was succeeded by Gelon. But the latter did not become **master of Syracuse** until 485. By unifying much of eastern Sicily and central-ising it on Syracuse, Gelon created the only power in Sicily capable of successfully resisting Carthaginian expansion, which he did at the Battle of Himera in 480 (166).

157–161. Much of the substance of these speeches is the product of H's literary imagination: the hyperbolic **with all the armies of the east** (157.1); the maxim that **well-laid plans have a prosperous issue** (157.3); the Homeric references and the Athenian claim to be **the only nation never to have left the soil from which it sprang** (161.3), are hardly relevant to the negotiations in hand but calculated to be popular with H's Athenian audiences. Finally, Gelon himself is made to use imagery, **the spring of the year . . . is lost** (162.2), which was ascribed by later sources to Pericles (Aristotle, *Rhetoric* 1.7.34,3.10; Plut. *Pericles*, 8.28.) Pericles, like Churchill, may have borrowed extensively from earlier sources, but the link here is probably between him and H rather than between Gelon and an unknown earlier lyric poet. As to the actual negotiations, there is no reason to doubt that Gelon made extreme demands for the leadership, which were to some extent vindicated by his success against the Carthaginians. It may well be that, like the Argives, but for reasons of future security rather than past disasters, he was unwilling to put his armed forces at risk against an external enemy.

165.1. Terillus . . . brought into Sicily . . . an army 300,000 strong from Carthage . . . : The number seems suspiciously inflated in order to match Persian numbers opposing the Greeks on land. The tradition seems firm, however, that the Carthaginian force, consisting as usual of mercenaries, was large and well-equipped. This in turn raises the question of whether its landing, while technically a response to Terillus' invitation, was in fact the wholehearted seizure of an opportunity for which the Carthaginian leaders had been waiting to exploit a split among the Sicilian tyrants. Later Carthaginian history confirms their abiding interest in the island, with its rich resources of grain.

166.1. The Sicilians also maintain . . . on the same day: The fact that H is following the Sicilian view of these events should be remembered when considering whether the coincidence was purely accidental or not. There is a tradition preserved by Ephorus (fr.111) and Diodorus Siculus (11.1, derived from Timaeus) of some form of cooperation, perhaps even a formal alliance, between Xerxes and the Carthaginians. Scholarly opinion is fairly evenly divided: Burn (306) follows How & Wells (II,201) in accepting it, but Hignett regards the silence of Herodotus as decisive (95–96), while Hammond (*A History of Greece* (Oxford,

1959) 269) writes: 'it is unlikely that Persia feared any reinforcement of Greece from Sicily, or that Carthage wished to see Persia conquer Greece and perhaps advance upon Sicily. Two further probability-arguments seem to support the latter view. H's Sicilian sources would surely have sought to magnify their achievement at Himera by adding the danger of Persian complicity, if there had been any; and the Persian armament was thought by Xerxes and his chief advisers to be more than adequate for its task without help from Carthage.

168.4. the prevailing north-easters or Etesian ('annual') winds blew in August-September for about forty days, and the Battle of Salamis was fought in late September. The Corcyreans were caught between two theatres of war, in Sicily and Greece, so their hesitation is hardly surprising. H's hostility towards them is patent (cf. 3.49–53), but Thucydides does not make the Corinthians reproach them with cowardice or treachery at this time in the famous debate between them (1.37–43).

170.1. The story goes that Minos . . . : The historical counterpart to the legendary anger of Minos against Menelaus' people (i.e. the Spartans or Peloponnesians) concerns the Cretan attempts at colonisation, which met opposition from Spartan settlers at Tarentum (founded 707/6), as H describes. Minos addressed his people as a god, as the Trojan War was **in the third generation after his death** (171.1). H is following Homeric chronology (*Iliad* 13.451ff.; *Odyssey* 19.178ff.)

172.1. The Thessalians did not submit to Persia until they were compelled: As Thessaly had no centralised government, it is unlikely that there was any unified direction of Thessalian politics. In deciding on their response, the Greeks must have considered **the intrigues of the Aleuadae** (7.6.2, 130.3), and whether **the Thessalian delegates** could guarantee their countrymen's support for the cause of Greek freedom, and indeed whether that cause meant anything to the Thessalians in comparison with their own self-preservation. Their decision to send north **10,000 Greek infantry** (173.2), a substantial force, was based on three principles: that it is better to fight as far as possible from one's homeland (Plutarch, *Themistocles* 7); that it was better to face the barbarian before he was joined by medising Greeks (including the Thebans); and that mountain passes afford inferior numbers a better chance of success than open terrain.

173.4. another way into Thessaly: H is surely right to prefer this reason, for by now the Greeks must have had some idea of Persian numbers, if not from the spies released by Xerxes (148.1), then

from other sources. The Greek position was even more vulnerable
than H describes: in addition to the pass near Gonnus, there were
two more distant but more easily negotiable passes to the west,
at Petra and BVolustana, which Xerxes probably used in his
advance. Defence of more than one pass would have required
more Greek infantry, and proportionally more Thessalian commitment to the Greek cause. Sparta's doubts about this and her own
reluctance to defend a distant outpost are reflected in their
appointment of **Euanetus son of Carenus ... not of the royal
blood** to lead their contingent. It may well be that H did not
realise, or did not wish to admit, the full extent of Persian
influence in Thessaly at this time. See Hignett, 102–103; Burn,
341–343.; and esp. N. Robertson, 'The Thessalian Expedition of
480 B.C.', *Journal of Hellenic Studies* 96 (1976) 100–120.

175.2. communication would be easy: Cooperation between fleet
and army was as essential to Greek strategy as it was to Persian.

176.3. to the south-west—inland ... other side of the roadway:
H actually writes **to the west ... to the east**, apparently not
realising that the direction of the road is east and west. But his
topography of both Thermopylae and Artemisium is otherwise
admirably clear, when allowance is made for later geological
changes.

177. Pieria: The country through which one approaches the
passes into Thessaly, north of Mount Olympus. The Greeks left
themselves with little time to spare.

178.1. Pray to the winds: Another piece of Delphic ambiguity,
made to serve a literary purpose by Herodotus, who, like a tragic
poet, foreshadows major events with minor ones and lays signposts for his audience. They may now hear of the defeat at
Thermopylae in the knowledge that a reversal of fortune is to
follow with the wrecking of part of the Persian fleet in a storm.

179. ten of the fastest ships were sent ahead both to look out for
the Greeks and to check that the waters were safe (cf. 183.2). This
first encounter may have begun after the Persians surprised the
Greeks at dawn in the harbour after a night approach (so Hignett,
160, following Munro in *Cambridge Ancient History* iv.285). But if
it took place in open water, the Persian success showed that their
ships were swifter and more effective than the Greek triremes in
such conditions, and must have influenced subsequent Greek
strategy.

181.1. Pytheas of Aegina reappears at Salamis (8.92). Leon of
Troezen was apparently sacrificed as the first-fruit of victory, but
H's reference to his name (= Lion) implies that he thought animal

rather than human association with bravery and ferocity were in his captors' minds. But human sacrifice was common among the Persians, Phoenicians and other barbarian races, so it is likely that the choice of Leon as victim was due to an unfortunate etymological association.

183.1. fire-signal: See also 9.3. The most famous literary appearance of beacons is, of course, in Aeschylus, *Agamemnon* 280ff. For details of their use in ancient times, see Polybius 10.43ff.

184.1. I find by calculation: This suggests that the numbers are not based on Persian records. H accepts the traditional Aeschylean number of 1207 for the Persian fleet, and the numbers of naval personnel stem from that, on the assumption that each ship had a full complement. The total for both ships and their complements is probably too high, but not as preposterously so as those for the land forces (see 7.61ff. notes). Most of the numbers are, on H's own admission, mere estimates.

187.2. 110,340 bushels should read 110067$\frac{1}{12}$. See H & W II,213–214. Xerxes is plainly represented as a tragic figure at the height of his power immediately before the first of his disasters.

188.1. in lines, eight deep: With prows facing out to sea, to make maximum use of the mooring-space available, as explained by Homer, *Iliad* 14.33–37, where the Achaean ships are similarly drawn up. If the storm created on-shore waves, this was the best direction for them to be facing, but much of the damage would have been caused by the ships falling foul of one another.

189.1. Boreas: A god whose power was of increasing concern to the Athenians from the early fifth century, when growing maritime trade took their ships north-eastwards to the Black Sea. Note H's scepticism here: there had been an earlier storm which was not explained thus, but he feels obliged to record Athenian opinion.

190.1. Four hundred ships: i.e. naval ships, excluding merchantmen (cf. 191; so at 236.2, where Achaemenes mentions only the fighting ships). The tradition that both the Delphians and the Athenians prayed to the wind-gods probably embodies a later belief that the storms inflicted very great damage on the Persian fleet. Herodotus, believing the original number to have been 1207, may have heard that the gods destroyed one in three of the barbarian ships, and so arrived at his estimate.

murder of his son seems to suggest that Ameinocles himself was the killer, but the killing was probably accidental. As a vignette illustrating the swift succession of triumph and disaster, the story probably reminded H and his readers of Croesus' tragic loss of his son after boasting of his wealth to Solon (1.29–45).

196. the horses of Thessaly were renowned throughout Greece. But the superiority of Persian cavalry to the best Greece could offer (the only other Greeks with cavalry comparable to the Thessalian were the Boeotians, who also medised) materially affected subsequent Greek strategy.

197.1. Laphystian Zeus: or Zeus the Devourer. The legend and the ritual described is one of the few survivals of human sacrifice in Greece, where in historical times it was regarded with religious aversion.

198.1. tide: Although the Aegean is for the most part tideless, quite strong ebb-and-flow currents occur in certain narrow channels and gulfs in the north (cf. 8.129).

Herodotus' rather sketchy account of Xerxes' march from Therma to Thermopylae (198–200) is to be explained by the fact that it was largely unopposed, and perhaps also by H's limited knowledge of the topography of the area; though he did visit it.

202. The discrepancy between the 3100 Peloponnesians listed here and the 4000 in the epitaph (228) written soon after the battle and not likely to be an exaggeration, must be due to omissions by H, perhaps of *perioeci* or of men from Elis. Their numbers were still very small for the task they faced.

203. The Locrians of Opus . . . all they had: Estimated at 1000 by Ephorus, making the non-Peloponnesian contingent also 3100. The Theban contribution of 400 is notably small.

204. Leonidas traced his descent: Genealogies like this were reserved for men of heroic distinction, in the Homeric tradition (e.g. *Iliad* 10.68). See 8.131,139; 9.64.

205.2. fathers of living sons: Explained sufficiently by national policy of preserving the families of pure Spartan stock (*Spartiatai*), whose male members formed the backbone of their army. The defence of the pass at Thermopylae was probably seen as a compromise by the Spartans, as by the other Greeks; but it was a compromise fraught with imponderables. The Greeks to east and north of the Peloponnese insisted on all-Greek defence of their land, but how many of them would remain steadfast? Nevertheless, the pass afforded a good chance that their loyalty would never need to be tested. Events proved that it could have been defended with a very small force, since treachery was needed finally to turn the Greek position. Hence the Spartan contingent of only three hundred, matched by similar numbers from other states, was sufficient to stop the Persian advance through the narrow passage, and the stand was made as part of a concerted plan to keep Xerxes out of Greece (176.2) without thought of failure or self-sacrifice. H perhaps did not make up his mind about Thermopylae. He and later historians (Diod. Sic. 11.4.3–4, following Ephorus) were influenced by the oracle which demanded the death of a Heraclid king as the price for the preservation of Sparta (220). Although this would have been satisfied by the death of Leonidas alone, it introduced fatalistic elements into the story, which were as attractive to historians as to contemporaries who sought excuses for the defeat. For the different views on the aims and motives surrounding the campaign, see Hignett 113ff., esp. 124–5.

207. It was proposed . . . : The Peloponnesian proposal to fall back on the Isthmus is rejected by Macan and Hignett as unhistorical. In noting Peloponnesian isolationism, however, H directs no criticism at Sparta.

208.3. combing their hair: One of many curious stories intended by H to underline the fundamental difference in outlook of Greeks and barbarians. The martial preparations of the Spartans, who wore their hair long, stem from a self-imposed discipline and willing patriotism. They also have a ritual quality: a battle is treated like a form of festival celebration (cf. Xenophon, *Spartan Institutions* 11.3; 13.8). The warriors' contemptuous disregard for the spy reminds us of Demaratus' prediction (102.3) that the Spartans would fight, whatever the size of the army opposed to them.

210.1. For four days Xerxes waited: The fact may be accepted, but hardly H's explanation, which merely follows on from the King's conversation with Demaratus. The Greek position was in fact formidable, and neither Xerxes nor his army had experience in the specialised techniques of attacking a well-defended superior position. The eventual attack, far from being ordered by Xerxes in rage, may have been intended to test Greek strength. In the meantime he may also have been awaiting a favourable outcome at sea, and when this was not forthcoming, decided that the Greek army must be overcome at whatever cost.

211. The Spartan superiority over the barbarians in both training and equipment is briefly but vividly described in this chapter. The feigned retreat followed by a counter-charge was intended to bring the enemy to close quarters, where the superior armament of the hoplites took its toll, especially if the front was narrow and enemy numbers could not be used to advantage. See 9.62 for further discussion of Greek and Persian weaponry.

213.1. How to deal with the situation Xerxes had no idea: It would have been surprising if he had not consulted his generals, but H represents him as acting alone, with no battle plan because he had thought there would be no battle; viewing the proceedings from afar, as at Salamis, and improvising tremulously as each new situation arose.

Ephialtes or Epialtes. Once the tradition was established that the army was betrayed by a Greek traitor, there were certain to be counter-accusations, but other authorities agree with H, who records the traitor's fate, complete with its twist of paradox, with satisfaction.

215–219. The track . . . : H's description of the Persian ascent is beautifully effective in its graphic simplicity, relying on paratactic sentence structure and precise use of tenses. He breaks off his narrative of the Persian march when they still have a long way to go (end of 219 . . . **with all possible speed**). H is following mainly a source sympathetic to Sparta, but Delphic influence is also present as he is somewhat dismissive of the Phocians (cf.8.29; 9.17–18). See Forrest, *art.cit.* (n. on 6.121) 7.

219.2. The army split . . . : Judgement as to which of the stories was true depends on one's estimate of the strength of Leonidas' authority. In 204, H says he is **in command of the whole army** while **The contingents of the various states were under their own officers**.

220.1. It is said . . . : The whole of this chapter is derived from Spartan sources anxious to affirm the authority of Leonidas, the resolution which Demaratus' account of the Spartan character would lead readers to expect, and the divinely-ordained inevitability of defeat. These stories found general acceptance, and Leonidas' stand was later praised even by Sparta's critics (e.g. Isocrates, *Panegyricus* 92). H is careful, in his usual manner, to mention the allegation that the Spartans were deserted by the other Greeks, and his earlier narrative, by referring to a **council of war** in which **opinions were divided** (219.2), seems to imply that Leonidas, in the last resort, did not have the power to compel his allies to stay and fight. Certainly they could not have detained the Thebans **as hostages very much against their will** (222), and Plutarch's indignation at this slander of his fellow-countrymen (*On the Malice of Herodotus* 31) is fully justified. But the Spartan tradition did not entail criticism of any other Greeks, and it suited her allies to accept her version of events. The oracle was probably a later fabrication devised to justify the smallness of the Spartan force.

224.1. as those of men who deserve to be remembered: These words recall the beginning of the *History*. The short narrative of the final encounter is rich in Herodotean themes: religious observance;

fatalism; the barbarian way of fighting, needing whips; the large numbers of the dead. The individual prowess of Leonidas and the bitter struggle over his body have clear Homeric models. The story of Dieneces and his famous remark probably arose from the tradition that the Persian archers administered the *coup de grâce*, an inglorious end made more palatable by the addition of the spice of a *bon mot*.

228.1. *Four thousand here from Pelops' land*: This number would need to include a thousand *perioeci* from Sparta, unless the writer is carelessly including the Thespians. See note on 202.

231. disgrace (*atimia*) involved not merely being 'sent to Coventry' but loss of civic rights generally (Xenophon, *Spartan Institutions* 9.4–6). At this time it was inflicted with rigour. Later, after numbers of *Spartiatai* had dwindled, (Xenophon, *Hellenica* 6.4.15), cowardice in battle and other derelictions were punished less severely (Thuc. 5.34.2; Plutarch, *Agesilaus* 30).

233.1. The Thebans: H is unreasonably hostile (see Plutarch, *On the Malice of Herodotus* 31). It is likely that their contingent under Leontiades comprised men who were unsympathetic to the medising party in power (Diod. Sic. 11.4) (cf. Thuc. 3.75, describing the despatch of Brasidas by the Spartan government with an army of Helots). Mention of the Theban **capture of Plataea** (233.2), which began the Peloponnesian War in 431 B.C., seems to point to a contemporary, probably Athenian source.

234.2. equals: *homoioi*, like *atimia* a term of special significance in the Spartan constitution. It described all males of pure Spartan stock (*Spartiatai*) who fulfilled their civic and military obligations. The following conversation contains an interestingly contrasting pair of strategic ideas, including the most explicit statement of Xerxes' amphibious plan of invasion (. . . **if fleet and army keep in touch and advance together** (236.2). The idea of occupying Cythera was more suited to a navy familiar with Greek waters, such as a roving Athenian fleet in the early years of the Peloponnesian war. It was no doubt a subject of discussion among H's Athenian friends, some of whom would have held naval commands. Hardly less interesting is the reference to Greek envy (236.1). It explains a difference between Greek and Persian attitudes. The Greek believes in divine envy of success, and reflects his belief in his own attitude; whereas the Persian enjoys his good fortune without inhibition. Finally, a point of resemblance is seen in Xerxes' remarks about the sanctity of guest-friendship, which is close to the Greek view.

Book 8: Artemisium and Salamis

Resuming his narrative of naval operations from 7.195, H shows as much interest in the political background as in the actual preparations for the battles at Artemisium. The numbers of ships supplied by each state are given in descending order, and this indicates the Athenian preponderance in the clearest possible way. Their patriotic altruism is thereby given the maximum recognition. But at this time Athenian naval prowess had yet to be proved. They may initially have laid claim to the naval command, but strong opposition was to be expected from states with a longer naval tradition, especially Corinth and her recent adversary Aegina. The idea that Athens was the natural leader of the Greeks at sea, and Sparta the leader on land did not gain currency until Athens had established her maritime empire through the Delian Confederacy. By referring briefly to the beginnings of that confederacy with the words **the Athenians made the insufferable behaviour of Pausanias their excuse for depriving the Lacedaemonians of the command** (3.2), H shows that he is seeing the events of 480 in the light of subsequent history. His verdict on Athenian imperialistic intentions after the Persian Wars is more positive than that of Thucydides, who says that the Athenians formed the confederacy after careful consideration of approaches from the Ionians (1.95.1–2), and that the Spartans were anxious to be rid of the war against the Mede (95.7).

4.1 Artemisium: The site of a temple of Artemis, not a town, on the northern coast of Euboea, some forty miles east-north-east of Thermopylae. By choosing this station the Greek fleet both protected Euboea and challenged Xerxes' strategy of close contact between his army and navy. See Hignett, 153–154.

things had gone very differently with the Persians: i.e. the storm had reduced the number of Persian ships by far less than they had expected. It is highly unlikely, in spite of the present and previous references to it (7.183, 192) that retreat from Artemisium was contemplated at command level. It suits H to introduce the idea once more as part of a story illustrating the character of Themistocles. Wily, resourceful, unscrupulous and corrupt, the Athenian leader held a special fascination for H. Though influenced by the hostility of most of his informants, he saw that Themistocles was the ablest of the Greek commanders.

7.1. they detached a squadron of 200 ships: H does not say precisely when the Persians did this. The plan to force a decision at Artemisium and destroy the entire Greek fleet (6.2) should have been conceived before the main Persian fleet arrived at Aphetae.

in which case this squadron would have been sent ahead of the main fleet. Sailing **outside Sciathus, in order to escape enemy observation** makes no sense for ships putting out from Aphetae, but good sense for a fleet sailing south-eastwards along the coast of Magnesia and past the east coast of the island.

8. Of the two items of news brought by **Scyllias**, the first amplified what the Greeks knew already (7.192) about the damage inflicted on the Persian fleet by the storms; but this and other stories told about the most renowned salvage-man of antiquity ensured that his name came into this part of H's narrative. It is characteristic of H to try to rationalise even the most preposterous tales.

9. they waited till the evening: Probably to give themselves the option of an early disengagement. Against superior numbers the Greeks intended the first encounter to be no more than a skirmish. See 11.2 n.

11.1. close circle: The counter to the *diekplous*, here translated as **tactics** because it had by H's time become a general term for battle manoeuvres. See note on 6.12.). The 'circle' required disciplined and coordinated seamanship, was primarily defensive in conception, and could win a battle only against a rash enemy. See Thuc. 2.83,89.

11.2. they set to work, and succeeded in capturing thirty Persian ships: One of the few solid facts in H's account, but it raises more questions than it answers. If the Persian fleet was large enough to surround the Greek 'circle', how did the latter not only escape but capture thirty enemy ships? The solution to the problem probably lies in Persian numbers: the first sea-battle did not involve the whole Persian fleet. The encircling line of their ships was comparatively thin and easily penetrated.

Salamis: One of the chief cities in Cyprus, not the island near Athens where the sea-battle was fought.

12–13. H's narrative has the colour and rhythm of epic poetry as he describes the raging of the elements. He concludes it with an unequivocal reference to divine intervention on the Greek side. The wind-god had answered their prayers.

14. fifty-three ships from Athens, together with the news . . . : H does not say that the ships brought the news, or that they were a detachment which had been sent to guard the Euripus channel (so How & Wells II,239). The effect which they had on Greek morale suggests that their arrival augmented the overall numbers of the fleet. They were probably recently completed and manned, and were sent as the final instalment of the Athenian contingent. Yet even with this addition to their strength, the Greeks still adhered to their strategy of engaging only parts of the Persian fleet, hoping thereby to whittle away their numerical advantage.

15. Xerxes . . . took the initiative . . . it so happened that these battles at sea took place on the same days as the battles at Thermopylae: They decided to engage the Greeks off the Euboean coast, perhaps on orders from Xerxes, whose advance was being held up. H's reference to the coincidence of the battles does not necessarily imply that he thought it purely fortuitous, as in the case of Himera and Salamis (7.166) and Plataea and Mycale (9.101.1–2). The latter part of this chapter, and the advice given by Achaemenes to Xerxes (7.236.2 and note), show that he had a firm grasp of the central strategic principle. By deciding to attack the Greek fleet in its chosen position, perhaps in modern Pevki Bay (see below), the Persian admirals were unable to exploit their superior numbers.

16.1. evenly matched: Not in numbers but in performance: hence the battle was a 'draw', but a moral victory for the Greeks because they were so much fewer. Such detail as can be gathered from H's short narrative of 'the most important sea-fight that had ever been fought in the Mediterranean' (Hignett, 189), suggests that the battle was fought in a more or less confined area, perhaps Pevki Bay, which favoured the Greeks. Perhaps H exaggerates the **confusion . . . caused by the ships fouling one another** (16.2), giving too little credit here, as elsewhere, to Persian seamanship. The short list of individuals whose prowess is praised (17) shows that he suffered from a dearth of informants. The **capture of five Greek ships** was carried out by the well-trained marines, and the Greeks clearly came out of the fighting in a shaken state. **They determined to quit their station and withdraw further south** (18), but did not actually withdraw until they had received the news from Thermopylae (21). This and other factors suggest that the Greeks were more in control of the situation than H seems to imply. See S. Sidebotham, 'Herodotus on Artemisium', *Classical Weekly* 75 (1982) 177–186. As at Salamis, Themistocles is the key figure in the story: in both cases he is faced with the wavering resolve of the Greeks, and tries to devise means of restoring it. In the present instance he is overtaken by events. The sequence of these is reasonably clear, but H may have misrepresented the mood of the Greek sailors because of bias against the navy (see Hignett, 190–191). Themistocles is apparently made to share their pessimism when he seeks to reduce the size of the enemy fleet by means of propaganda directed towards the Ionian and Carian contingents. Yet even when he fails to persuade them, the Greek commanders subsequently risk an even larger part of their combined forces in another sea-battle. In these chapters H is perhaps too preoccupied with recording the machinations, real and imaginary, of Themistocles.

23.1. The Persians refused to believe it: H does not say when the Persians at Aphetae heard the news from Thermopylae, which would have explained the Greek naval withdrawal.

24–25. Was Xerxes' action propaganda or merely an example of his naive vanity? H would probably want his readers to choose the latter alternative, but the concealment of his dead was only an incidental touch. What was important was the fact that he had annihilated an army containing some of Greece's finest fighting men, and in view of his own vast resources his losses offered little assurance to other Greeks who might be planning to oppose him.

26.2–3. Tritantaechmes, son of Artabanus assumes his absent father's role, warning his fellow-leaders of the extraordinary character of their enemies. The contrast between Persian materialism and Greek idealism is a recurrent Herodotean theme. See S. Usher, *The Historians of Greece and Rome*, (London, 1969 and Bristol, 1985), 11–12.

27.1. Thessalians . . . had always been on bad terms with the Phocians: A normal relationship between neighbouring states in Greece. For this enmity, see 7.176.4; Pausanias 10.1. H adopts a neutral position, regarding the enmity of Phocians and Thessalians as a typical example of Greek disunity and perversity, as he implies in his remark : **If Thessaly had remained loyal, no doubt the Phocians would have deserted to Persia** (30.1). But the sources of the stories in these chapters seem to be Phocian rather than Thessalian. They were no doubt gathered at the same time as H heard the Delphic temple-legend which told of the repulse of the invading Persians from the temple precinct. This story he now tells, simply allowing full play to his narrative powers and revelling in a tale of an awesome divinity overpowering a presumptuous human transgressor of its domain. It was too good a tale to qualify by introducing personal opinions as to its accuracy. It also served to enliven what would otherwise have been a rather uneventful narrative of the Persian advance, especially that of the main part of Xerxes' army which advanced through Boeotia, most of whose cities readily surrendered. The march through Boeotia to Attica took about eight days.

40.2. They had expected . . . they learned: Such expectations would have been unrealistic after Thermopylae, whatever the Peloponnesians may have promised before. Once the decision had been reached to withdraw southwards, there were too many ways into Greece for them all to be defended. The Isthmus, with Salamis nearby, was the natural place to establish a combined front to meet the enemy. H is influenced by the Athenian point of view in this part of his history. By representing the evacuation as improvised and unexpected, he puts the Peloponnesians in the worst light; but it is likely that, when **the Athenians . . . . issued a proclamation that everyone in the city and countryside should get his children and all the members of his household to safety as best he could** (41.1), contingency plans had already been drawn up. Certainly prior agreement must have been reached with their prospective hosts at Aegina, Troezen and Salamis.

41.2. The Athenians say that the Acropolis is guarded by a great snake . . . they believed so literally in its existence . . . : This popular belief seems to have persisted (Aristophanes, *Lysistrata* 758. Even in Plutarch, *Themistocles* 10, where its behaviour is said to have been exploited by Themistocles, with the help of the priests of Athena Polias, in order to accelerate the evacuation, the snake's existence is not doubted. To H all that mattered was that the people believed in it.

42.1. the fleet was larger . . . : By 54 ships; and nine new states contributed. See How & Wells II,248. Corinth contributed 40 ships. The contingent from Megara numbered 20 (8.1.1). The items he lists add up to 366, but he states twice (48 and 82.2) that the total, before two later additions, was 378. The solution to the discrepancy offered by How & Wells (II,249) centres on the Aeginetan contingent. They contributed 30 ships, but an undisclosed number **were employed in guarding their own island** (46.1). H & W suppose that this number was 12, and that they subsequently joined the main fleet. But Herodotus states clearly that **their best *thirty* were the ones which fought at Salamis** (46.1).Attempts to make H's figures tally precisely should probably be abandoned. But the catalogue, even if it is not completely accurate, on the whole inspires confidence, being free from the exaggerations of the Athenian contribution found in later sources (Thuc. 1.74.1; Demosthenes, *On the Crown* 238). As to the total number, H must have been faced with conflicting pressures from his informants: a general wish to magnify the glory of the victory by exaggerating the odds against them, and a desire that the contribution of their own states should be fully, even generously represented. In particular, states which had suffered losses at Artemisium were nevertheless anxious that posterity should not assume that they played a smaller part at Salamis. Hence there is some room for suspicion of numbers stated to have been the same for both battles (those of Athens, Corinth, Megara, Chalcis and Eretria).

49. at Salamis, a council of war was held: H turns only briefly to the council at Salamis before describing the capture of Athens, but long enough to record that it had already been decided to abandon Attica. The later reaction of the same Greek commanders to the news of the fall of the Acropolis (56) is therefore surprising: what had they expected? (This description of double exposure to disaster is H's way of showing the full measure of the difficulty Themistocles faced in persuading the Peloponnesians to fight east of the Isthmus. It is even possible that many Athenians were not yet fully reconciled to the abandonment of their city: hence the psychological effect of its capture. See A.R. Hands, 'On Strategy and Oracles 480/79', *Journal of Hellenic Studies* 85 (1965) 56–57; and in general J.F. Lazenby, 'The Strategy of the Greeks in the Opening Campaign of the Persian War', *Hermes* 92 (1964) 264–284, esp. 279ff.

H's narrative of the capture of Athens is straightforward, but lacks chronological data. All he says in the course of it is that in the siege of the Acropolis **for a long time Xerxes was baffled** (52.2). But previously he has said that the defenders were not fighting troops but **temple stewards and needy folk** (51.2); and even while describing their unexpectedly stout resistance remarks that **Their wooden wall had betrayed them** (52.1), suggesting that the issue was as good as decided soon after the defenders had made their gallant decision, based upon a misinterpretation of the oracle given in 7.142. Thus 'a long time' may in this context mean 'a longer time than so small and weak a force might have been expected to resist'. On the other hand, the only stimulus that might impel Xerxes to hasten a final confrontation was the change of the seasons, which was still some way off. He could afford to wait for a few weeks and hope for dissension in the Greek ranks. In the meantime the forlorn garrison on the Acropolis presented no threat, and could be contained and perhaps starved into submission. This may be closer to what actually happened, but H cannot be expected to record such an ignominious end.

55. this olive . . . had sprung from the stump: Chosen as the tree to symbolise the life of the state, this olive had many scions growing throughout Attica. Because of the tree's extraordinary powers to survive the ravages of fire and the axe, it was forbidden to uproot the stumps of these sacred olives. See Lysias 7 *On the Sacred Olive*. The appearance of fresh shoots after fire is entirely possible, though perhaps not **on the very next day.**

56. Meanwhile at Salamis the effect of the news . . . was so disturbing: See n. on ch.49 above. Once the Persians were in Attica (50), which **had already been given up** (49.1), the occupation of the city should have caused no new surprise. But it may well have happened as debate among the Greek leaders was reaching a crucial stage and hence added to the size of Themistocles' task of persuasion. This was already enormous: if we follow H's narrative, there was no agreement at this stage that Salamis would be the site of the deciding sea-battle; on the contrary, the majority were on the point of confirming an earlier decision to fight **in defence of the Peloponnese** (49.2).

57.1. an Athenian named Mnesiphilus: One of the earliest sophists (Plutarch, *Themistocles* 2), who taught his fellow demesman Themistocles oratorical skills; but here surely used by H's hostile sources to minimise his part in the vital decision to fight at Salamis. See F.J. Frost, 'Themistocles and Mnesiphilus', *Historia* 20 (1971) 20ff. Thucydides (1.138.3)and other later writers, including Lysias, Plato and Xenophon, had a better opinion of Themistocles' originality and statesmanship, and even from H's account his grasp of the essential strategy of keeping all available Greek forces together is clear enough. H at least gives due credit to his persuasive powers, and puts the tactical arguments in his mouth, leaving only the political considerations to Mnesiphilus.

59. Themistocles . . . was interrupted by Adeimantus . . . the Corinthian: Hostility to Corinth is a recurrent feature of H's account of the Salamis campaign. Mutual hatred may well have been of recent origin at that time, following the expansion of the Athenian fleet from 483 B.C. until it exceeded that of Corinth by the outbreak of the war. Hence it was natural that this hatred should be expressed through recriminations about naval activities. Their enmity intensified after the Athenian alliance with Megara (Thuc. 1.103,4), and was still strong when H was at Athens.

60. Themistocles' speech, addressed nominally to Eurybiades because the final decision rested with him personally as supreme commander, sets out proposed actions and probable consequences antithetically, in the manner of a formal deliberative oration, and is therefore one of the earliest examples of that genre in literature. Characteristic of such oratory is the introduction of generalisations about human behaviour, here exemplified by the last sentence **Let a man lay his plans with due regard to common sense, and he will usually succeed; otherwise he will find that God is unlikely to favour human designs** (60 c). As a qualification of H's religious determinism, suggesting that man, rather than God, is responsible for giving his projects a reasonable chance of success, this is an important statement.

62.2. Siris in Italy: Near the site where the Athenians founded Thurii in 443 B.C., where H lived for a number of years. He may have died there. See pp.12–14. Athenian interest in colonising the west manifested itself from time to time in the fifth century, and culminated in the ill-starred Sicilian Expedition of 415–413 B.C.

64.2. sent a ship to Aegina for Aeacus himself and his other sons: i.e. sent for their images. Ajax and Telamon were grandson and son of Aeacus respectively. The other sons of Aeacus were Peleus, father of Achilles, and Phocus. Their territorial connections with Salamis are obscure, so H may have confused the relationships. In 5.80 'the sons of Aeacus' seem by their clear connection with Aegina to be Telamon and Ajax.

65.1. There is a story . . .: For H the story serves the purpose of foreshadowing a major change of fortune, with supernatural forces playing their part. In his desire to enhance this element, H allows to pass without comment the doubtful statement of Dicaeus that **There is not a man left in Attica**. It is quite possible that a group of Athenians travelled the short distance from their place of refuge in Salamis, in order to hold the festival that celebrated the rebirth of nature in the Attic countryside. This would have been encouraged by their leaders as an excellent morale-booster before the great struggle. Powell *ad loc.* seems perverse to deny any connection between this epiphany and the Eleusinian Festival, since both Dicaeus and H himself make the connection by implying that this was the normal time for its celebration.

66.1. In my judgement the Persian forces both by land and sea were just as strong . . . : After describing Persian naval losses of around 700 ships in Northern Greece (7.190,194; 8.11,13,14,16), and stating that the god was doing all in his power to make the Persian fleet equal to the Greek or not much larger (8.13), H now says that the fleet was back to its former strength. He does this in order not to contradict the popular tradition preserved by Aeschylus (*Persians* 341) which he had used earlier (7.89.1) and which glorified the Greek achievement to the highest degree by numbering the Persian fleet at 1207. His attempt to rationalise this discrepancy by adding reinforcements from small towns and islands fails in the face of probability. On land, however, it is entirely possible that the comparatively small Persian losses could have been replaced.

68.1. Artemisia owes her prominence in this suspiciously brief debate and later to H's determination to portray the weakness of Persian counsel and resolve. Only a woman has the courage to give Xerxes good advice, and in the course of it she ironically uses sexual comparison inversely when she says **the Greeks are as far superior to us in naval matters as men are to women** (68 a 1). Later, in the heat of the battle (88.3), Xerxes is made to comment: **My men have turned into women, my women into men.** Perhaps H has paid undue attention to the queen who ruled in Halicarnassus in his youth, whose version of events may have been one of the earliest he heard, and whose powerful personality offered literary possibilities when H came to write his history. But her advice to Xerxes seems too perfectly prophetic, corresponding too neatly with the actual course of the battle, and on the political side echoing the opinion of likely Greek behaviour ascribed to Mnesi-philus (57.2).

70.2. The Greeks were in a state of acute alarm, especially those from the Peloponnese: As before Artemisium, according to H, though there the panic affected the whole fleet (8.4.1). Here he appears to sympathise with the dilemma facing the patriotic Peloponnesians, emphasising their feeling of insecurity by noting that **Of these seven peoples all the communities except the ones I mentioned remained neutral in the war — which, to put it bluntly, is as good as saying that they were on the Persian side** (73.3). The Argives in particular were suspected of medism.

74. The Greeks at the Isthmus . . . while the Athenians, Aegine-tans and Megarians still maintained that they should stay and fight at Salamis: By drawing this clear distinction, H modifies his picture of Greek panic. The ships from these states made up more than half the fleet, and Aegina had a further number in reserve (46.1). Of the Peloponnesians, only Corinth had a significant navy. Their attitude is presented ambivalently by H, but even if they favoured a naval engagement, the remaining states were in the majority in the Congress, which appears to have operated on a 'one state one vote' system. Hence, Themistocles was right to fear **that he would be outvoted** (75.1). The story that follows appears in a different form in Aeschylus *Persians* 355–60, not naming Themistocles or Sicinnus but 'a Greek man from the Athenian camp', whose message is simply that the Greek fleet was contemplating flight during the night. The important assumption behind both stories is that Xerxes was determined to engage the Greek fleet wherever it was; and this assumption is confirmed by the outcome of his own council (69.2). But the stories also serve to explain why Xerxes decided to make his fatal move *when* he did, and to supply him with reasons for expecting victory in unfavourable conditions. It would be very curious if H, who has gone to great lengths to portray the overweening self-confidence of Xerxes, should make him the victim of a trick rather than of his own vainglorious folly if the story of that trick were untrue. Most authorities reject it as part of the Themistocles-legend. For discussions of the problems see How & Wells II,379–381; Hignett, 403–408. The story is accepted by J. Hart, *Herodotus and Greek History* (London, 1982) 98.

77. Now I cannot deny that there is truth in prophecies: H's attitude characteristically combines reason with religious belief. See Usher (1970) 18.

holy shore of Artemis: This could refer either to the eastern shore of Salamis or to that of Attica near Mounichia, since both were sites of temples of Artemis.

79.1. Aristides . . . had been banished: By the device of 'ostracism', introduced at Athens, probably by Cleisthenes, not as a punishment for wrongdoers but as a means of preventing damage to the state caused by rivalry between leading men. Aristides' ostracism in 483/2 had been the result of his losing a political battle with Themistocles, perhaps over the latter's naval programme. H makes his own contribution to the glowing tradition of Aristides' probity and patriotism, which was upheld especially by his aristocratic friends. These qualities are pointedly contrasted with the untrustworthiness of Themistocles (80). Aristides seems to have resumed a leading position quickly, but it is to be noted that H does not say that his return from Aegina was also his return from exile. A decree recalling exiles was passed as early as June 480 (see [Aristotle], *Athenian Constitution*, 22.8 and Rhodes *ad loc.*), so that Aristides could have returned and stood successfully for office, perhaps that of *strategos*, by this time (September). This is suggested by the fact that he leads a body of hoplites in the capture of the Persian garrison on Psyttaleia (95), and later at Plataea (9.28).

83.1. a comparison of all that was best and worst in life and fortunes: This use of antithesis and generalised philosophical themes in a deliberative speech, together with its apparent division, concluding with a 'winding-up', marks this speech of Themistocles as an early example of Athenian hortatory oratory and its author as a pioneer in that genre; unless, of course, Herodotus is guilty of anachronism.

84.1. The Greeks checked their way and began to back astern: Probably as part of a deliberate manoevre to draw more and more enemy ships into a confined space, in accordance with the plan of

The Battle of Salamis, 480 B.C.

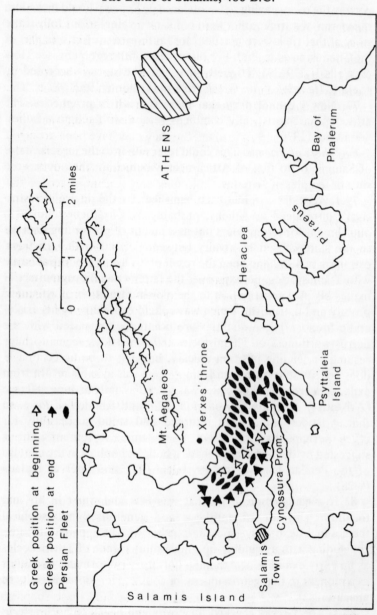

Themistocles (60 a). Much of H's account now centres on the fortunes of individuals, some of whose descendants were his chief informants on the battle. For the topography see W.K. Pritchett, 'Towards a Restudy of the Battle of Salamis', *American Journal of Archaeology* 63 (1959) 251–260; A. Masarrachia, 'La Battaglia di Salamine in Erodoto', *Helikon* 9–10 (1969–70) 68ff.

85.1. The Athenian squadron . . . left wing on the western, Eleusis, end of the line: i.e. left from the Athenian standpoint. The Greek line faced north, the Persians south with the Attic coast at their backs. The size of the Athenian fleet meant that they occupied a large part of the line; but they may have been arranged in depth at the western end of it, because it was here that the greatest strength was needed in order to restrain the advance of the incoming Persian ships into the only vacant space in the channel. It was on this restraint that the strategy of compression and congestion depended.

86. the Greek fleet worked together . . . the Persians . . . were no longer fighting on any plan: Confirming that the Greeks were fighting to a definite plan. As to the Persians, the supervisory presence of **the king's eye** had a positive effect on the course of the battle, prompting his ship-captains to press forward incoordinately in quest of glory. After giving way initially, allowing the Persians to crowd into the channel, the Greeks hemmed them in against the northern shore under the horrified gaze of the King, causing them to fall foul of one another. As is clear from ch. 87, which otherwise probably gives a misleading impression of space available for manoeuvre, ramming played a major part hin the battle, and many men died in the water, speared like tunnies (Aeschylus, *Persians* 424–426). H tries to deal impartially with the deeds of both sides, but appears to have obtained more detailed information from Carian court sources than from the Athenians. Unfortunately, members of the losing side are usually in a poor position to explain the strategy of the victors.

91. The Aeginetan squadron: They operated on the Greek right, and were detached from the main fleet in the closing stages. Their task of catching and destroying the fleeing enemy called for greater combative prowess and seamanship than the static slaughter of the enemy in the main battle-area. Hence their reward of the first prize (93). H's knowledge of this seems to have prompted him to seek further information from Aeginetan sources, and these supplied him with the stories in 91–92. For earlier charges of medism made by the Athenians against the Aeginetans, see 6.49.

94. The Athenians have a story: The fiction of Corinthian flight arose from later enmity between the Athenians and Corinthians, following the Athenian alliance with Megara (Thuc. 1.103.4). Focus on the part played by Adeimantus in this and other phases of the campaign may be a later refinement of the story, arising from the effective part played by his son Aristeus in the revolt of Potidaea immediately prior to the Peloponnesian War (Thuc. 1.60; see also 2.67). Perhaps the most obvious weakness of the story is the failure to explain where Adeimantus fled to, when both east and west ends of the Salamis channel were blocked by enemy ships. One suggestion is that the Corinthians were sent to confront the Egyptian squadron which was guarding the western entrance (Diod. Sic. 11.17); but whatever task they were given, they fought bravely in the Greek cause, as epitaphs and most of their countrymen attested.

95. Aristides' capture of **Psyttaleia**, in the later stages of the battle when the Greeks had won control of the sea on at least one side of the island, is described at some length by Aeschylus (*Persians* 447–464) in order to give the hoplite class a share of the victory.

97. the extent of the disaster: H has no figures for losses, and those given for the Persian side could have been no more than rough estimates. They are given as 500 ships by Ctesias and over 200 by Diodorus, who says that the Greeks lost 40 ships.

98.1. Persian couriers: These were used only for royal and official dispatches. Their speed and efficiency is confirmed by Xenophon (*Cyropaedia* 8.6.17–18), who emphasises their importance as a means of communication in a large empire. H's comparison with the Athenian torch-relay introduces the idea of fire, and he may have been thinking of Aeschylus, *Agamemnon* 282, where the famous beacons announcing the capture of Troy are described as *angariou puros* ('of fire the post-rider').

99.1. Xerxes' first dispatch . . . the second, however: H refers back to 8.54, but delays describing the reception of his first dispatch until now, in order to give maximum impact to the effect of the second. Aeschylus' description of the mourning that followed the news of Salamis at Susa (*Persians* 517ff.) was no doubt in H's mind, but he enjoyed freedom from the restrictions of time and space that shackled the dramatist, and used that freedom to good effect to draw on earlier events. **Laying the blame on Mardonius** (99.2) refers to the debate in 7.5.9, but it must be doubted whether the Persian populace knew of Mardonius' part in influencing Xerxes. H is providing Mardonius with motivation for continuing the war and fulfilling his **hope of becoming governor of**

Greece himself (7.6.1), while at the same time depicting the scene of frenzied Oriental grief and concern for the safety of the King. Artemisia, this time cast in the role of compliant counsellor, advises him to exploit his paramount position, but Mardonius furnishes two arguments of greater substance, firstly when he says **None of the reverses we have suffered have been due to us** (100.4), and Xerxes quotes him as saying **my army and my Persian troops, who have not been responsible for any of our recent disasters, are anxious to prove their worth** (101.2); and secondly when he refers disparagingly to the **Egyptians and Phoenicians and Cyprians and Cilicians**, and says **Persia is not involved in their disgrace** (100.4). The important implication of these statements is that Persian operations in Greece should henceforth be military rather than naval. Instead of contesting the command of the sea, Persia would concentrate on trying to neutralise Greek naval supremacy through diplomacy.

102.3. you will be going home with the object of your campaign accomplished—for you have burnt Athens: Another reference to the initial debate (7.8 b 1), but the same speech of Xerxes contains clear indications of wider territorial ambitions (7 a 2).

105–106. Hermotimus, his chief eunuch: Greek and barbarian ideas clash in this story of mixed fortunes culminating in terrible revenge. The employment of eunuchs in Oriental courts was normal at this time (see e.g. 3.92); but Hermotimus and Panionius were Carian and Ionian Greek respectively. Even the cruel tyrant Periander (3.48) did not castrate the 300 Corcyrean boys whom he sent to the court of Alyattes to become eunuchs, and the Samians who ingeniously rescued them showed the same Greek revulsion for the practice as does H in the present passage.

107.1. That day . . . the same night: If the decoy operation described in 97 took place while Xerxes conferred with Mardonius, this action may have taken place the following day, i.e. two days after the battle. The speed of the King's departure evidently surprised the Greeks (108).

109–112. The only probable facts to be drawn from these chapters are the Greek pursuit of the Persian fleet as far as Andros, where they received some form of payment from the Andrians and other islanders and returned home. For the action as an ominous foretaste of Athenian imperialism, see Lenardon, p. 86. The rest of the narrative is tainted with anti-Themistoclean legend, adapted by H to illustrate his special characteristics— adaptability, eloquence, foresight, cunning and greed. His message to Xerxes (110.2) may be historical (it is apparently accepted by Thucydides (1.137.4)), but since it serves only to encourage Xerxes in the retreat on which he is already embarked, its concern is mainly with Themistocles' subsequent career, and for that reason alone it should be suspected. Acceptance of this message automatically rules out acceptance of Themistocles' message to Xerxes before Salamis (75): there must have been limits to the King's gullibility. Most implausible of all is the statement **Themistocles' idea in saying this was to lay the foundation for a future claim on Xerxes** (109.5). As Forrest says *(art.cit. n.* on 6.121): 'It is quite inconceivable that on the morrow of Salamis Themistocles was looking ahead to about 467.'

113.3. 300,000 men: The number should probably be scaled down in proportion to earlier exaggerations. Hignett (267) suggests 60,000.

114. satisfaction (= requital, justice): An important word in an important chapter. The idea that 'justice' (*dikê*) means different remedies to the different parties in a dispute is the central theme of Aeschylus' *Oresteia*, and especially the *Agamemnon*. For H it also serves to foreshadow the outcome of the Plataea campaign, while the part played by Delphi reasserts the idea that the gods were on the Greek side.

115–120. Xerxes' retreat by land is less harrowing in H's account than in that given by Aeschylus (*Persians* 485–513). The alternative story (118) owes its inclusion solely to H's principle of 'telling all'. When he says **I do not find this second account of Xerxes' return at all convincing** (119), we are reminded that he does not profess to believe the stories he tells (7.152.3).

121. Warships . . . to be dedicated . . . at the Isthmus . . . at Sunium: Both, appropriately, to Poseidon.

122. three gold stars: One surmounting the mast and representing Apollo, the other two perhaps representing the Aeacidae, whose images were sent for before the Battle of Salamis (8.64). These heroes were more grandly immortalised in the pedimental sculptures on the Temple of Aphaea, now in the Glyptothek at Munich.

123.1. prize of valour: The circumstances of this award are puzzling, and the story has a Homeric ring about it. There was no recent precedent, as the combined forces of Greece had not faced an external foe since the days of Agamemnon.

123.2. The commanders met at the altar of Poseidon to cast their votes: The men, the place and the procedure all indicate that this was a meeting of the same Congress whose deliberations plotted the course of the war from its beginning (7.172.1 and Hignett, 98).

124.2–125. he went to Lacedaemon . . .: The purpose of
Themistocles' visit to Sparta was probably not merely honorific,
though the Spartans had good reason to be grateful to him for his
cooperation in the matter of the leadership and for the success of
his naval policy. Their more perceptive statesman would have seen
advantages in the continuance of that policy, and discussion of its
future implementation may well have taken place at Sparta during
his visit. It was probably this policy, rather than resentment at his
friendship with Sparta, that his political opponents at Athens used
to undermine his popularity when he returned. His political eclipse
was not quite as rapid as his virtual disappearance from H's pages
suggests (he is mentioned only once more, in 9.98.4): in his
building of the city fortifications after the war he displayed all his
earlier diplomatic finesse (Thuc. 1.90–91); but soon afterwards his
enemies had their way, and he was ostracised (Plutarch, *Themistocles* 22).

126–129. Potidaea was the key to the peninsula of Pallene now
that Persia no longer held command of the sea. Scione sent troops
to her aid because the cities of Pallene had formed an alliance. The
combination of narrow passage and flat coastal ground can pro-
duce remarkable tidal effects in the otherwise tideless Mediterranean. Cf. 7.198.1. H's account of this episode is self-consistent
and clear, as his statement of belief in divine retribution (129.3).

130. A chapter of discordant statements. The intention that his
fleet should henceforth play a purely defensive role was consistent
with Xerxes' decision (8.103) that the remainder of the war should
be fought on land. The question of the fleet's morale (**so far as
naval operations were concerned, the Persians had completely lost
heart** (130.3)) is therefore largely irrelevant, and the idea it
contains of a Persian view of the situation independent of the
King's will, as if his admirals (he Persians enjoyed a degree of
autonomy, is surely unhistorical.

131.2. Leotychides . . . traced his descent back to Heracles:
Tradition synchronised the Dorian Invasion with the Return of the
Heraclidae, and both branches of the Spartan royal house traced
their ancestry to Hyllus, son of Heracles. For the Agid (senior)
branch, see the pedigree of Leonidas (7.104). Their latest common
ancestor was Aristodemus, the grandfather of Agis and great-
grandfather of Euryp(h)on, son of Sous (hence the name Eury-
pontidae for Leotychides' branch, and its junior status because
Euryp(h)on was the nephew of Agis. For genealogy as a Homeric
mark of honour, see 7.104 n.

131.3. Xanthippus married into the Alcmaeonid family and was father of Pericles.

132.2. Strattis, the master of Chios since Darius' Scythian expedition (4.138), was, like other Ionian despots, a puppet of the Persians.

132.3. Samos . . . as far away as the Pillars of Heracles: These were the modern Straits of Gibraltar. This is a gross exaggeration of the attitude of the mainland Greeks, especially of the Athenians, to Ionia. H may here be voicing Ionian prejudice, or seeking to provide maximum dramatic preparation for the coming invasion of the Ionian coast.

134.1. to pass the night in the temple: In the hope of being visited and enlightened by the god in a dream (Aristophanes, *Plutus* 669–671). Trophonius and Amphiaraus were local Boeotian earth-gods, and as such did not have the universal fame and political connections of Delphic Apollo. Mardonius may nevertheless have thought that responses from them favourable to his cause would consolidate the loyalty of medising Greeks æin Boeotia and Central Greece that was an essential preliminary to his new campaign.

135.3. the god's response had been delivered in Carian: Did the oracle wish to conceal its answer from the Thebans? For explanation of this mysterious story perhaps the best starting-point is Mardonius' (apparently) consequent action. He made overtures to the Athenians, for the very good reasons given. They, then and later embarrassed at his approaches, wanted it to be known that he was inspired to make them not by medisers from their own city but by an oracle. A possible reason for concealing the oracle's message from the Thebans might have been fear that knowledge of it would weaken Theban loyalty to Mardonius, who would be seen by them as courting their enemies. Oracles notoriously took short-term political views, and this one may have thought that medism was the best policy for Boeotia at this time, and did not wish to see it undermined.

136.1. Alexander, the son of Amyntas was admired by H, who took pains to establish the Greek origins of his family (5.21). His credentials as a mediator could hardly have been better: on the one hand, he had arranged the murder of Persian envoys to his father's court (5.19–20), concealed the fact (5.21), and married his sister to Bubares, son of the satrap Megabazus.

137–139. On the Royal House of Macedon, whose later scions included Philip II and his son Alexander the Great, see G. Cawkwell, *Philip of Macedon* (London, 1978), 21–26. In this story the resourceful and ambitious Perdiccas symbolically claims the whole of his master's estate by accepting the hearth and calling the sun to witness.

140–144. In his account of these tripartite negotiations, H skilfully combines the realism of tough diplomatic bargaining with some of his most forthright praise of Athenian patriotism. Their objective, given that submission to Mardonius was unthinkable, was to secure wholehearted Spartan cooperation with their own strategic objectives, which required that the Cithaeron-Parnes line rather than the Isthmus should be defended against Mardonius, i.e. that the Greeks should **meet him in Boeotia** (144.5). It was in order to obtain this cooperation that they delayed their reply to Alexander until anxious Spartan envoys arrived. This enabled them to make a convincing display jof their own resolution, but also to point out that even their most determined efforts could not withstand another Persian invasion by land. But H also provides unifying motivation on a more idealistic level with the Athenian affirmation of common Hellenic religion, ancestry, language and institutions (144.2). It is one of the most memorably patriotic passages in Greek literature, and a fitting prelude to the final struggle with the barbarian on Greek soil.

Book 9: Plataea, Mycale and the End of the War
1. The leading families of Thessaly continued to maintain their previous attitude . . . they urged the Persians to the attack: Fearing reprisals in the event of a Greek victory. As before (7.172.1) H singles out the leading families as the medisers in Thessaly.

2.1. There was no better place . . . to encamp . . . but, with Boeotia as his base: The advice of the Thebans, like that of the Thessalians, was prompted by self-interest. But it was more subtle and contained both strategic and tactical elements: Boeotia bordered Attica, and was therefore the best place from which to exert diplomatic pressure. It was also suited to the use of cavalry, if the Greeks should decide to initiate hostilities.

3.1. Mardonius . . . His whole heart was set: A poetical stock-phrase of H for barbarian leaders' irrational lust for territorial conquest (cf. that of Croesus, 1.73.1). But Mardonius' decision to reoccupy Attica was logical, intended to reduce the odds against him by knocking Athens out of the war and perhaps intimidating some of the other Greek states into submission. It also served to keep his troops occupied and to maintain their morale.

3.1. beacons: see 7.183n. For a detailed discussion, see the edition of Book 9 by E.S. Shuckburgh (repr. Cambridge, 1954) 79–81.

5. Lycidas (Cyrsilos in later sources): His fate was cited in later literature as an illustration of the Athenian patriotic temper at this time, their finest hour (Demosthenes, *On the Crown* 202–204; Lycurgus, *Against Leocrates* 122). Its summary severity also reflects feelings of fear and uncertainty, which made men intolerant and free speech dangerous.

6. sent a message: Delivered by highly-placed envoys, according to Plutarch, *Aristides* 10 — Cimon, son of Miltiades, Xanthippus and Myronides.

some means of helping themselves: Perhaps a veiled threat of medism, (see 11.1 below), but at this stage of negotiations more likely a reference to Themistocles' threat to remove the population of Athens on ships to Siris in South Italy (8.62.2). H never lets the Athenians appear irresolute, but he presents different levels of resolve: in 7 a (below) he makes the Athenians say **we shall never willingly make terms with the enemy**, whereas in 8.144 they have said **we will make no peace with Xerxes so long as a single Athenian remains alive**.

7.1. the time of the Hyakinthia: A festival of Apollo held in June.

the wall . . . was almost finished: It was built about six miles east of Corinth.

8.1. The Ephors: These five annually elected 'overseers' organised all aspects of executive government in Sparta, including the reception of foreign envoys. From this passage it is clear that they also had considerable emergency powers. On the ephorate, see H. Michell, *Sparta* (Cambridge, 1964) 118ff., esp.123.

H's account of a long Spartan delay, caused by selfish isolationism and ended by a secret despatch of troops, does not in itself fully reveal the factors that affected their deliberations. As so often happens, we have to look elsewhere in his narrative for the missing clues. They are to be found in the following chapters (12, q.v.)

9.1. a Tegean named Chileus: This man's advice is probably a literary device rather than a historical fact, designed like that of Mnesiphilus to Themistocles (8.57–58) and that of Themistocles to Xerxes (8.75) to discredit the recipient of it. The ephors must already have been aware of the strategic principles which it embodied (8.59–60), and the Isthmus wall had probably been completed some sixth months previously (8.71), so that it constituted no new dimension to Peloponnesian security in the summer of 479.

Both sides had their own reasons for fighting a decisive land campaign, and as soon as possible: on the Persian side because they were far from home with insecure lines of supply; on the Greek side because of the danger that the confederate forces would disperse if there were no action as the season advanced and harvests were to be gathered. As to the location, neither side wanted to fight in Attica because it afforded narrow avenues of retreat for both, and from the Persian viewpoint it was **bad country for cavalry** (13.3).

12. The Argives: It is their hostility to Sparta and consequent medism (7.148.2) that provides at least a partial explanation of her leaders' reluctance to send an army out of the Peloponnese, and for the secrecy surrounding its departure. The commitment of Elis and Mantinea to the Greek cause was also in some doubt.

15.1. Mardonius . . . began his withdrawal from Attica into Boeotia, by the eastern route.

15.3. The position he occupied: Note that H describes two fortified positions: the present one, probably on both sides of the Asopus river, and a more strongly walled inner palisade on the north side of the river only ('in Theban territory', 65.1).

16.1. Thersander is one of only four oral informants named by H (2.55.3; 3.55.2; 4.76.6). His story was particularly opportune from an artistic point of view, foreshadowing the fateful campaign yet followed immediately by a description of the Greek forces which joined Mardonius, apparently increasing his prospects of success. The story may well have had divided Persian counsels as its background (see chs. 41,66); but .its fatalism, so characteristic of men whose lives are in the hands of others, was very much to Greek sixth- and early fifth-century taste.

17.1. The Phocians were a defeated people, their land occupied. But the fact that their enemies the Thessalians (8.28–31) had embraced the Persian cause rendered them unreliable, and indeed some of them fought for Greece (31.5). Perhaps the incident in the mountains above Thermopylae (7.217), when a Phocian contingent retreated to the heights in the face of a sudden attack, led Mardonius to think that their courage needed to be tested as well as their loyalty. Again, the force of 1000 here described was apparently recruited following the re-occupation of Phocis (Hignett, 197). H uses the word *sphodra* ('positively') in describing the Phocian action. This is very revealing, implying as it does that H placed higher value on loyalty than on pure patriotism. Thus the Phocians, though they despise the barbarians, will fight steadfastly on their side once they have committed themselves.

The promise of material reward no doubt confirmed their resolve: Phocis was later one of the main breeding-grounds for Greek mercenaries.

19.3–20. (The Greeks) occupied the lower slopes of Cithaeron . . . Mardonius sent his cavalry: As the Greeks chose their position in order to be above the enemy and away from the plain, where they feared that Persian cavalry might be used against them with devastating effect, Mardonius' tactic was to try to tempt them to leave that position. But it is scarcely likely that they would oblige him, and the Megarians were in danger only while they were moving to a more permanent position. H recounts this minor incident because it is his only opportunity to highlight an Athenian action. H's source for this story may have been Lampon the soothsayer, who was a co-founder of Thurii, where H spent his later years. Olympiodorus may have been his father or uncle. The Athenians may well have volunteered, but the presence of archers in their contingent would have made them Pausanias' natural choice for this task.

22–24. H makes the most of the Athenian exploit by drawing particular attention to the Homeric struggle of **the three hundred Athenians, fighting alone** (23.1) over Masistius' body before the arrival of other troops. From the Persian standpoint, the failure of their cavalry to make an impression on the massed Greek hoplites was a more disturbing omen for the outcome than the death of Masistius. It encouraged the Greeks to take up a position on the plain which gave them access to water and was probably less than a mile from the city of Plataea. See G.B. Grundy, *The Topography of the Battle of Plataea* (London, 1894): like Herodotus, Grundy explored the battle area thoroughly; W.J. Woodhouse, 'The Greeks at Plataea', *Journal of Hellenic Studies* 18 (1898) 33–59; J.A.R. Munro, 'The Campaign of Plataea', *Journal of Hellenic Studies* 24 (1904) 144–165; H.B. Wright, *The Campaign of Plataea* (New Haven, 1904); A. Boucher, 'La Bataille de Platées d'après Hérodote', *Revue Archaeologique* 2 (1915) 257–320; W.K. Pritchett, 'New Light on Plataea' *American Journal of Archaeology* 61 (1957) 9–28.

26.1. one of the wings: i.e. the left wing, since the Spartans as leaders were on the right, as at Salamis (8.85). For a full discussion of the second Greek position, which was downhill and to the west of the first position, see Hignett, 301–310. By moving down to a more exposed position nearer the Persian camp, Pausanias hoped to provoke a Persian attack and conclude the campaign quickly. An early result was also in Mardonius' interests. Yet in H's account eight days pass before battle is joined.

The speeches of the Tegeans and Athenians are literary pre-cursors of the great ceremonial (*epideictic*) orations of Pericles and the Attic Orators Lysias, Isocrates, Demosthenes and Hyperides, though they are written in a simpler and more natural style. H sees to it that the Athenians have the better of the argument, repre-senting them as the champions of just causes and of Greeks against foreigners, rather than merely doughty fighters. This is more appropriate to the present situation than the Tegeans' emphasis on their victories over their neighbours, and the speech's subject-matter interestingly corresponds quite closely with that of later Athenian epideictic oratory, including Pericles' Funeral Speech in Thucydides 2.35–46, which contains references to exploits in the recent as well as the distant past.

27.5. So let us leave ancient history out of it . . . Marathon . . . stood alone: Perhaps not surprisingly, the Athenians exaggerate their most recent success, as do later panegyrists (e.g. Isocrates, *Panegyricus* 86). The Plataeans fought at their side at Marathon (6.111); and it was Xerxes' host that contained **forty-six nations**, not the expedition under Datis and Artaphernes.

28–30. The Greek numbers given by H are accepted by most modern authorities. The most notable absentees are from the cities of Arcadia, traditionally a rich source of fighting men but here represented only by Tegea and Orchomenus. The Lace-daemonian contingent reflects the domestic ratio of 7:1 by which Helots outnumbered *Spartiatai* (full Spartan citizens). The **34,500 others** are included by H on the assumption that each hoplite was attended by a lightly-armed auxiliary, but this custom might vary in different states.

H probably exaggerates both the Persian and the Greek num-bers serving under Mardonius at Plataea. If they had outnumbered the patriotic Greeks by about three to one, the course of the battle, even if it had ended in a Greek victory, would have been more protracted and complicated than his account of it suggests. Moreover, ancient land battles in which smaller armies defeat much larger ones usually involve some brilliant manoeuvre on the part of the former, and none such seems to have been devised at Plataea.

33.2. came within a single event: Rather, 'came within one throw', referring to the last of the three throws in the wrestling event (*palê*) which decided the Pentathlon after the contestants had tied 2–2 in the first four events (long jump, discus, javelin and sprint).

33.4. Tisamenus saw that the Spartans were extremely anxious to get his support: On the strength of the Delphic Oracle, and also no doubt of the ancient reputation of the Iamid family as soothsayers, claiming descent from Apollo. Soothsayers came into their own in times of war and other crises. The Spartans were among the most religious of the Greeks, never crossing their borders without making sacrifices and receiving favourable omens. Their kings, who combined religious and military functions, normally performed these sacrifices. In attempting **to induce him, by the offer of a wage, to become joint leader with their Heraclid kings in the conduct of their wars**, the Spartans were not offering Tisamenus a permanent kingship, which was obviously a far greater honour than the full citizenship which he demanded, but trying to take advantage of the divine honour which he apparently enjoyed by appointing him chief priest. Hence for "wars" (above) we should probably read "pre-campaign sacrifices". For a similar story having a religious context, involving seemingly unreasonable demands increasing after each refusal but finally being met, compare the story of the acquisition of the Sibylline Books by Tarquinius Superbus (Dion. Hal. 4.62.1–4; Zonaras 7.11.1).

34.1. Argives . . . women who had all gone mad: Driven so, like Pentheus in Euripides *Bacchae*, for refusing to take part in his celebrations (Apollod. 2.2.2), the three daughters of Proetus, king of Tiryns, left the city and were joined in the wilderness by other Argive women. Melampus cured them with hellebore, was married to one of Proetus' daughters, and received one third of the kingdom.

35.2. at Tegea . . . at Dipaees: These battles established Spartan supremacy in the Peloponnese after the Persian Wars, and should probably be assigned to the years 473–471. See A. Andrewes, 'Sparta and Arcadia in the Early Fifth Century', *Phoenix* 6 (1952) 1–5. The Messenian War (Thuc. 1.101.3–103.1), fought against a mainly Helot population, ended probably in 459. (On the chronological difficulties see A.W. Gomme, *A Historical Commentary on Thucydides* (Oxford, 1956) 401–408). The Battle of Tanagra (Thuc. 1.108.1) was fought in 457.

36–37. The similar **omens** for both sides account for the delay of up to ten days before the battle, and H takes the opportunity to digress with stories about the two soothsayers. Their advice closely corresponds with the strategic demands of the situation: both sides were better equipped to fight in the position they had taken up rather than on the ground held by the enemy. The area around the Persian camp was more suited to the deployment of cavalry, which included mounted archers, than the Greek position.

38.2. Mardonius . . . would be able to cut off a great many of the men: An assignment ideally suited to his mounted archers, attacking columns of infantry on the march. With the **continual influx of men**, Mardonius faced a real danger of being outnumbered, so their impending arrival must have been a major factor in his decision to attack. The anti-Theban bias is strong in this chapter.

41–42. There is some confusion in these chapters arising from H's desire to portray Mardonius like Xerxes as manically impetuous, ignoring good advice, sacrifices and prophecies, all set against the historian's instinct to present a rational side to his deliberations. But it seems strange for H to describe Mardonius as **irked by the protracted inactivity** (41.1) after giving a cogent reason—**the Greek forces were rapidly increasing**—why he should join battle immediately. H feels he must stick to the standard literary formula which he has followed before previous momentous decisions: the tragic warner gives his advice, and it is rejected. Artabazus merely repeats the advice offered by the Thebans in 9.2.

42.3. sack the temple at Delphi . . . keep away from the temple: The first part of the prophecy had already been fulfilled in intention by the earlier Persian advance on Delphi (8.35ff.), when only divine intervention prevented the destruction of Apollo's shrine. That story and the present one may be two separate explanations offered at different times by the Delphic authorities for the temple's escape from Persian pillage. The present one adds a familiar ingredient to H's picture of Mardonius—the arrogant despot's idea that he can avert the realisation of a prophecy, here spiced by his error in identifying it.

43.1. The Encheles achieved victory over the Illyrians by following the oracle's advice to take as their leaders Cadmus and Harmonia (Apollod. 3.5.4), who had been expelled from Thebes by the Argives (5.61). The story represents a historical tradition connecting Thebes with the ruling chieftains of Southern Illyria.

44–45. The story of the nocturnal visit of **Alexander** to the Athenian camp serves the purpose of exonerating him from later charges of medism and of justifying later Athenian good will towards his state, but it may be historical. Less credible are the pre-battle manoeuvres of Spartans, Athenians and Persians (46–47): H's source for them is patently anti-Spartan. (See, for example, 54.1: **the Spartan habit of saying one thing and meaning something else**). Some of his aristocratic Athenian friends, sought to conceal the secondary role played by the previous generation of their hoplites at Plataea by harking back to Marathon and disparaging the Peloponnesians who bore the brunt of the Persian assault. Pausanias' handling of the whole army prior to the battle could hardly be more critically described, though the criticism is not personalised. Mardonius' taunt (48) adds a touch of Homer, whose heroes often preface combat with an exchange of insults (*Iliad* 5.627ff.; 13.445ff.; 20.153ff.; 21.139ff.).

49.2. The Persian cavalry . . . spoilt the spring of Gargaphia: A major turning-point, causing the Greeks to retreat to a new position closer to Plataea. But the suggestion of a disorderly and unplanned retreat (52) is wholly unconvincing. Surely the plan was to lure the Persians over the Asopus (59.1) into territory more suited to the Greek hoplites than the Persian cavalry, and so fulfil the prophesy of the oracles that the side fighting from a defensive position would prevail (36); and that plan was followed faithfully.

53.2. the Pitanate regiment: A possible clue to H's source for this story. He conversed with Archias of Pitana when he visited Sparta (3.55.2). The wilful behaviour of this man's fellow-villager may be a 'camp tale' (How & Wells II,331), but there could well have been heated discussion of the strategic as well as the moral implications of a retreat. At all events, the delay is historical, and critically important for the course of the battle, which began when the Persians caught up with the withdrawing Spartans.

54. The Athenians, meanwhile, being well aware . . . : H makes their excuse for not moving until the rest of the army had begun to retreat a shade too contentious. No doubt there was some suspicion and rivalry between the Greek states. But there is some indication that the retreat of the different contingents was conducted according to a concerted plan, with the Spartans and Athenians following different routes to a rendezvous.

57. at a leisurely pace: The calm and ordered retreat of Amompharetus, which is reminiscent of the comportment of Sir Francis Drake on Plymouth Hoe, is a fitting prelude to a battle in which the discipline of the Spartan infantry plays such a prominent part. H is happy to return to his Spartan source at this point.

58. Mardonius' overconfident reaction to the Greek withdrawal is in character, but H's account clearly suggests that he had good reason for believing that they were in general retreat. But the ill-discipline of the Persian advance bodes ill for their chances.

60. The content of Pausanias' message makes reasonable sense from his point of view. The brunt of the Persian attack, headed by cavalry, seemed to be directed against the Spartans and Tegeans under his command on the right wing, and he could probably not

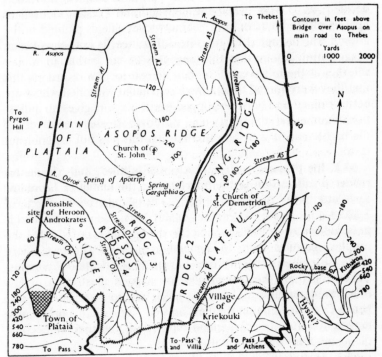

The Battlefield of Plataea (from *Xerxes' Invasion of Greece* by C. Hignett
© OUP 1963)

see the rest of the Greek forces. Athenian archers would certainly
have alleviated his discomfort, but he must surely have sent
messages to other contingents as well. H's concern is to establish
the *intention* of the Athenians to join in the decisive phase of the
battle. His difficulty in trying to describe the Athenians' part
sympathetically is compounded by the fact that their chief opponents in the battle were the Thessalians, who were friends of
Athens during his sojourn there (Burn, 535).

61.2. The Lacedaemonian number of **50,000** included seven
lightly-armed helots for each *Spartiates*, so that the latter

numbered about 6,000. Pausanias' tactics were to endure the volleys of arrows passively, relying on shields and armour, until the Persian infantry came to close quarters. Hence his judicious use of sacrifices to delay his side's action. The main engagement, fought on the Greek side by the Spartans and Tegeans, was decided, as H says, when the conventional Persian method of fighting pitched battles from behind wicker shields planted in the ground was disrupted by the Greek hoplites. It may thus be no exaggeration to say that the flimsiness of the barbarian wicker shields was the initial cause of their defeat, for it was through this that they were forced to join in close combat with men who were better-trained and better-equipped for it. Since H gives no indication of numerical superiority, and moreover stresses the bravery of the barbarians, it is to be assumed that this was not a significant factor.

64.1. the prophecy of the oracle was fulfilled, and Mardonius rendered satisfaction to the Spartans for the killing of Leonidas: Two utterances of the Delphic oracle should be recalled. In 7.220.3–4 the death of Leonidas or the destruction of their land is presented as an alternative choice to the Spartans, but in 8.114 the prophet instructs them to demand 'reparation' (*dikas* cf. here *dikên* (sing., 'satisfaction') from Xerxes for the death of Leonidas. Taken together, the two oracles are a good illustration of H's religious determinism: Leonidas must die to save Sparta, and hence Greece; while on the Persian side Xerxes in his pride must inevitably refuse the demanded reparation, and thereby become the agent of his own downfall.

64.2. Arimnestus died some fifteen years later.

65.1. the holy precinct of Demeter is identified by Grundy and others with the church of St. Demetrius. H's verdict on Pausanias' achievement in the battle, however much he tries to magnify the exploits of the Athenians, is in the end quite unequivocally expressed in the words **the most splendid victory that history records** (64.1).

66.1. Artabazus: Mardonius trusted him in spite of their disagreements, and probably intended that his corps of 40,000 men should form a second wave of attack. Artabazus continued his career with success, retaining Xerxes' favour (8.126). As satrap of Dascylium in 478–7 he assisted the intrigues of Pausanias that led to the Spartan king's ruin (Thuc. 1.129).

67–69. The Thebans shine in the reflected glory of the Athenians in H's narrative; otherwise Mardonius and his Persians are the only serious combatants of the invaders' side. This has the unhappy effect of leaving the rest of the Greeks, apart from the Spartans and Tegeans, unhonoured and unsung.

70.2. they have never mastered the art of attacking defensive works: Spartan weakness at siegecraft was related to their aversion to long campaigns and to their rigidly disciplined method of fighting. Their military system was organised with the maintenance of their supremacy in the Peloponnese as its main object. Knowledge of this weakness prompted the Athenians to build walls around the Acropolis after the Persian Wars (Thuc. 1.89–93), and later the Long Walls down to the Piraeus (Thuc. 1.108.3). These were later a major factor in the prolongation of the Peloponnesian War, which was finally decided at sea.

with the arrival of the Athenians: Courage, perseverance and improvisation rather than any specialised skills seem to have been their virtues. It may have been their success here and at Mycale (102.3) that earned them their later reputation. See Thuc. 1.102.2 and Gomme's note (I,301–2).

70.5. The Greek losses given here by H do not include the 600 from the left centre who were killed by the Theban cavalry (69.2), and they seem too small to square with his description of the fighting (**many of their men were killed** (61.3) . . . **many casualties in the Lacedaemonian ranks** (63.1)). H probably derived his Athenian figures from monuments, but failed to realise that these were tribal, and that no single inscription recorded all the Athenian dead.

71.2. Aristodemus: On his earlier exploits see 7.229–231.

72.1. Callicrates, the handsomest man in the Greek army: His death recalls that of Nireus in Homer, *Iliad* 2.673.

73.2. to recover Helen: The reference is to a myth involving Theseus, the founder of Athens, in an abduction of Helen before her marriage to Menelaus. It may have arisen to explain the worship at Athens of Helen's brothers, the Dioscuri, who were said to have rescued her.

73.3. raids . . . left Decelea unharmed: i.e. the five invasions between 431 and 425 B.C. Decelea was occupied by the Spartan king Agis in 413 on the advice of Alcibiades (Thuc. 6.91.6).

74–80. In these chapters H provides artistic relief from battle-narrative. They contain some of his favourite themes: tall stories of valorous deeds which have their rational counterparts (cf. Scyllias the diver in 8.8.3), a suppliant woman of aristocratic birth (a frequent figure of tragic drama) chivalrously treated by the Greek commander, who also refuses to vie with the barbarians in barbarity. Choice of Lampon the Aeginetan as the villain of the story may indicate Athenian prejudice against his state, which also appears in the statement that the **Aeginetans . . . laid the foundation of their future wealth** (80.3) by tricking the Helots rather than through the mercantile success which they had already enjoyed for many years, and which H has mentioned earlier (2.178; 4.152; 7.147). See also 85.3 (H & W II,325).

81.1. the three-headed bronze snake: Actually three intertwined serpents. As the list of states includes some that did not fight at Plataea, the monument was probably intended to commemorate victory in the whole of the war. Remains of it survive in the Hippodrome at Istanbul.

82.2. Pausanias . . . could hardly believe his eyes: Since his subsequent career was shortened and ruined by his addiction to the oriental life-style (Thuc. 1.130), there may be an element of irony in this story. On the other hand, H thinks highly of Pausanias, emphasising both his patriotism and his military prowess and underplaying his medism (5.32; see H & W II,12; Hignett, 343 n.7).

84–85. The information and the references to his inquiries here and elsewhere in H's narrative of the *Plataika* suggest that his researches for this crucially important part of his story were among the most thorough that he conducted, and included much topographical work.

86. The destruction of Theban power was a natural demand on the part of Sparta's allies the Athenians, Plataeans and Thespians. But at the end of an arduous campaign the Spartans were anxious to return home, and were ready to accept the Theban compromise provided that it satisfied their allies' honour. The surrender of their leaders and their losses in battle greatly weakened the Theban oligarchy.

89. Artabazus: H had informants who enabled him to follow Artabazus' career in some detail (See H & W II,276–7). His disengagement at an early stage of the battle (66) made his arrival in Thessaly before the Thessalian cavalry possible (*pace* H & W II,327), since the latter were apparently engaged in combat with the Athenians (31; 61) at an advanced stage of the battle. H has no fault to find with Artabazus, who represented prudent counsel and had been against facing the combined Greek forces on the plain of Plataea (41).

90. H resumes his account of naval operations from 8.132. The Persian fleet was at Samos. Both fleets were immobilised by fear. The Samian envoys appear to have had the solid support of their fellow-citizens, unlike the Chian exiles who had approached

Leotychides earlier (8.132). This fact may have weighed more strongly with him than the name of their leader. The coincidence of Plataea and Mycale is impossible to verify, and may be suspected when the same is alleged of Himera and Salamis (7.166). Plataea and Mycale both took place in early August, but were probably separated by several days, with Mycale the later. The Greek fleet numbered 110 ships when it assembled at Aegina in Spring 479 (8.131.1). It was this comparatively small number and uncertainty about Persian strength that made them initially hesitant. That the Greek leaders had agreed that naval operations should take second place to the effort against Mardonius is clear from the numbers of their land forces under arms prior to the battle of Plataea. Consequently Leotychides was faced with a tricky logistical problem, which was compounded by lack of information about the enemy's numbers and intentions. H is no doubt right to make the Samians disparage both, but Leotychides is unlikely to have believed them if he knew that the Phoenicians were still present in the enemy fleet. It is perhaps safer to place the dismissal of the Phoenicians (96.1) soon after Salamis, as does Diodorus (11.19), or to follow Hignett's suggestion (252) that the Samians were the bringers of the news of the departure of the Phoenicians, and that this news encouraged Leotychides to seek a naval engagement. The Persians, by contrast, sought to ensure that any battle should take place on land, with themselves in a defensive position behind fortifications. This was a surprisingly pusillanimous decision if their army really did number 60,000 (96.2).

98.2. All gear—boarding-gangways and so on— necessary for a naval engagement: Leotychides intended to fight in the old style rather than by manoeuvring and ramming. This raises the question of the extent of Athenian presence and influence. Were there too few Athenian captains and oarsmen who were competent to execute such manoeuvres, and/or too little Athenian influence at command level? The political situation at Athens probably provides the answer. The naval policy of Themistocles å,was in temporary eclipse, and the Athenian commander at Mycale was his opponent Xanthippus, who shared Leotychides' preference for traditional fighting methods. This proved providential at Mycale, where the Athenian hoplites played a significant part; and the force as a whole, in spite of inferior numbers, was well equipped to mount the land assault which Persian strategy imposed upon them.

98.2. Leotychides . . . appeal to the Ionians who were serving with the enemy: Themistocles had done the same before Artemisium

(8.22), but Leotychides had better reason to expect success. Samos, the most powerful Ionian state, was now without a Persian garrison: others would need little encouragement to follow their lead. It is likely that Persian suspicion of widespread Ionian insurgency dictated their ultra-defensive strategy based on land.

100.1. a rumour flew through the ranks: The fervid atmosphere of the battlefield was seen as a potent medium for the spread of rumour from Homer onwards: *Iliad* 2.93ff.; Aeschines, *Against Timarchus* 128, *On the Embassy* 144; Pausanias, 1.17.1. Its occurrence at Mycale is the strongest argument against the coincidence of the two battles.

102.1. The Athenians . . . the Lacedaemonians: Their respective routes of advance were probably dictated by the initial positions assigned to them in the line—the Athenians on the left, the Lacedaemonians on the right, as at Plataea. For the topography, see Hignett, 255–256. If the Athenians marched along the shore and the Spartans took an encircling path inland, the Greeks must have landed to the east of the Persian position and advanced westwards.

H's description of the battle itself is clear. The Persians planned to provide themselves with two lines of defence by first coming outside their fortified camp and fighting behind **a barrier of interlocking shields** (99.3). This plan was defeated by the closeness of the pursuit by the Greek hoplites after they had broken this first line.

103–105. There may be traces of Ionian propaganda in these chapters: the statement that **this day saw the second Ionian revolt from Persian domination** (104) certainly exaggerates the part played by the Ionians in the victory. But they, like the Athenians, were ever anxious in later years to match the military achievements of the Peloponnesians in the war against the barbarian. The bias of literary sources may also be at work. Historians of the period who were either Athenian or sympathetic to the Ionians and Athenians tended to favour the hoplite tradition because of their own background. Hence the prominence given to Marathon and the reluctance to accord Salamis, a battle won by the lower classes serving in the fleet, its proper importance. Mycale provided these historians with another glorious hoplite victory and the opportunity to celebrate, though with much less justification, another Athenian hoplite triumph. The reader of H's account, and of the narrative of the Ionian historian Ephorus of Cyme, as preserved by Diodorus Siculus, may therefore suspect that the Peloponnesians' part was greater, and that of the Ionians and

Athenians less, than they are represented by these historians.

106. Victory brought a critical moment of decision which set the course of Hellenic history for the next century. H presents the extremes of opinion that could have been held about the **future of Ionia**. Some scholars have doubted whether such a pessimistic view of the tenability of Ionia could have been held by Greek leaders. Yet it was one which might come naturally to the isolationist Spartans; while projects of wholesale transplantation to distant sites had been considered before (1.170) and even implemented (6.17, 20). Nevertheless it seems unlikely that after so decisive a victory serious proposals along these lines were made, not least because the Ionians themselves would have rejected them. H has magnified them in order to emphasise Athenian commitment to Ionian freedom, and to explain the enthusiasm with which the Ionians joined in the formation of the Delian League, whose first members, apart from Athens herself, were **the Samians, Chians, Lesbians and other island peoples who had fought for Greece against the foreigner**. H shows clearly how the League began as a naval alliance against Persia.

107–113. The story of **Xenagoras** the Halicarnassian leads H back to barbarian affairs after following Greek fortunes to their final victory. Now, as his mighty epic draws to its close, he chooses to leave his audience with some final thoughts about life and morals in the absolutist empire of Persia. The story he tells has the rich flavour of oriental court intrigue, with its stock ingredients of lust, greed, deceit and cruel revenge. The princess Artaynte, the central character, is the familiar tragic figure, **who must have been doomed to come to a bad end** (109.2) (see E.R. Dodds, *The Greeks and the Irrational* (Berkeley, Los Angeles, 1951) 56, n.55). The similarity of these concluding chapters to the early chapters of Book I suggests an overall ring-plan which affirms the unity of the *History* and places the responsibility for the war firmly on the Persian side by focussing on the royal court, the dynamic source of policy and action, and exposing the dangerous instability of its despotic inmates. The idea of royal women exerting such influence, and of one of them even wearing the king's robe, will have confirmed H's readers in their belief in the corruption and decadence of the barbarian empire.

114–121. The siege and capture of Sestos is represented as a purely Athenian enterprise by H, whereas Thucydides says that they were assisted by the Ionians (1.89.2). Although the Delian League had not yet formally come into existence, Thuc. makes this combined operation of its earliest members the first offensive action that led to the growth of Athenian power. Unfortunately H is too interested in the activities of the villainous Artayctes (see also 7.33), whose story involves the Homeric hero Protesilaus and hence introduces links between the Persian and Trojan Wars, which H could not resist (cf. 1.3–5.1). H ends the episode as he began it, following the movements of the Athenians. Hostilities were in fact renewed the following spring by a combined force led by the Spartan victor of Plataea, Pausanias, who completed the conquest of the Hellespontine region with the capture of Byzantium.

122. Far from being out of place or curiously anticlimactic, as has been suggested, this chapter explains with extraordinary succinctness the cause of the Persian defeat. It is scientific. The theory that the characters of the different races of men are determined by the climate and terrain in which they live was propounded in the Hippocratic tract entitled *Airs, Waters and Places*, 24. It also has a moral dimension: the Persians had the choice of remaining tough by staying in their harsh homeland, but elected to taste the luxuries first of Media, then of Lydia (1.71). Finally, they committed the fatal error of defying natural law by trying to conquer men who had not been exposed to the debilitating effects of luxury (9.82). Some Athenians, contemplating the glories of their newly adorned city before the beginning of the Peloponnesian War, might have found a warning hidden in H's last chapter; while at Thurii, H's adopted city, the citizens had the ruins of Sybaris close at hand to remind them of the terrible fate that may await people who let themselves become softened by wealth.

Bibliography

HERODOTUS

(a) **Monographs**

S. Benardete *Herodotean Inquiries* (The Hague, 1969)

C.W. Fornara *Herodotus*; an Interpretative Essay (Oxford, 1971)

T.R. Glover *Herodotus* (Berkeley, 1924)

J. Hart *Herodotus and Greek History* (London, 1982)

H.R. Immerwahr *Form and Thought in Herodotus* (Cleveland, 1966)

J.L. Myres *Herodotus, Father of History* (Oxford, 1953)

K.H. Waters *Herodotus the Historian* (London & Sydney, 1985) (containing the best modern bibliography)

(b) **Commentaries**

W.W. How & J. Wells *A Commentary on Herodotus* (2 vols. Oxford, 1912, repr.1928)

R.W. Macan *Herodotus, Books 4–9* (4 vols. London, 1895–1908)

Commentaries on individual books include those of E.S. Shuckburgh (Book 6: 1889; Book 8: 1903; Book 9: 1893 repr.1954) and J. Enoch Powell (Book 8: 1939 repr. 1956). Preeminent among modern commentaries is that of A.B. Lloyd on Book 2 (3 vols. Leiden, 1975–).

THE GRECO-PERSIAN WARS

A.R. Burn *Persia and the Greeks* (New York & London, 1962, 2nd edn. 1984)

G.B. Grundy *The Great Persian War and its Preliminaries* (London, 1901 repr. 1969)

P. Green *The Year of Salamis 480–479 B.C.* (London, 1970)

C. Hignett *Xerxes' Invasion of Greece* (Oxford, 1963)

R.J. Lenardon *The Saga of Themistocles* (London, 1978)

J.A.R. Munro chs. 9 and 10 in *Cambridge Ancient History iv* (1926)

GENERAL WORKS ON GREEK HISTORY AND HISTORIANS

A.R. Burn *The Lyric Age of Greece* (London, 1960; pbk. 1978)

J.B. Bury & R. Meiggs *A History of Greece* (4th edn. London, 1975)

J.B. Bury *The Ancient Greek Historians* (London, 1909 repr. New York, 1958)

J.K. Davies *Democracy and Classical Greece* (Fontana pbk. 1978)

V. Ehrenberg *From Solon to Socrates* (London, 1968)

M. Grant *The Ancient Historians* (New York, 1970)

N.G.L. Hammond *A History of Greece* (Oxford, 1959)

O. Murray *Early Greece* (Fontana pbk. 1980)

R. Sealey *A History of the Greek City States 700–338 B.C.* (Berkeley, 1976)

S. Usher *The Historians of Greece and Rome* (London, 1969 repr. Bristol, 1985)

H.D. Westlake *Essays on Greek Historians and Greek History* (Manchester, 1969)

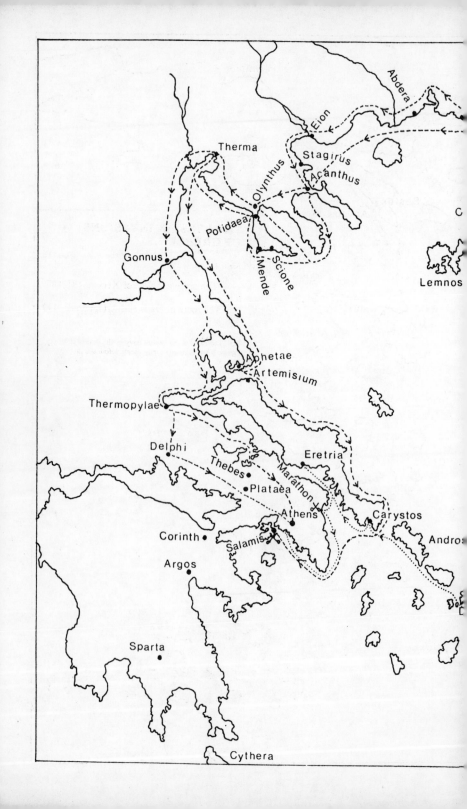

THE PERSIAN INVASIONS
OF GREECE

Scale: 48 miles = 1 inch

----The army and fleet of Xerxes, 481-480

...... The route of Datis and Artaphernes, 490

N.B. The route of the Persian navy in 480 begins at
Doriscus on the map: its movements before this are not
known

Maronea

Doriscus

Aenus

Perinthus

e Sarpedon

Cyzicus

Sestus

Abydus

Troy

Antandrus

Adramyttium

Atarneus

Sardis

Chios

Cydrara

Ephesus

Colossae

Samos

Cape Mycale

os
r.

Naxos

Halicarnassus

Rhodes